WHEN WE SWUNG
FROM CHURCH BELLS

WHEN WE SWUNG
FROM CHURCH BELLS

*Stories That Shape Our Faith
and Faith That Shapes Our Stories*

⸻

Callie Rebekah Feyen

FOREWORD BY Xan Morgan

RESOURCE *Publications* · Eugene, Oregon

WHEN WE SWUNG FROM CHURCH BELLS
Stories That Shape Our Faith and Faith That Shapes Our Stories

Resource Publications
An Imprint of Wipf and Stock Publishers
199 W. 8th Ave., Suite 3
Eugene, OR 97401

www.wipfandstock.com

PAPERBACK ISBN: 979-8-3852-6063-8
HARDCOVER ISBN: 979-8-3852-6064-5
EBOOK ISBN: 979-8-3852-6065-2

Scripture quotations taken from The Holy Bible, New International Version®, NIV®. Copyright © 1973, 1978, 1984, 2011 by Biblica, Inc. Used with permission of Zondervan. All rights reserved worldwide. www.zondervan.com

Jeanne Murray Walker gave permission to use the poem "The Voice" from *Pilgrim, You Find The Path By Walking,*

To the Misfits: may Grace disturb us all enough to turn us into stories for another day.

If you can't make something out of a little experience, you probably won't be able to make it out of a lot."

—Flannery O'Connor, *Mystery and Manners*, 84.

Contents

Contents

Foreword

SOME STORIES YOU READ. Others, you experience. Callie Feyen's newest work, *When We Swung from Church Bells: Stories that Shape our Faith and Faith that Shapes Our Stories,* undoubtedly falls into the latter category. From the moment you turn the first page, you'll find yourself drawn in, compelled to keep reading, not just for the engaging prose, but for the invitation her words extend.

Callie's storytelling is a masterclass in tenderness, honesty, humor, and delight. She creates a space where you are not only invited but *welcomed* to bring your whole self to a playful dialogue – not just with her stories, but with yourself and with God. Within these pages, you'll discover the freedom to wonder, to laugh until your sides hurt, to shed a quiet tear, to cringe in relatable moments, and ultimately, to feel profoundly seen. As Callie shares her experiences, you'll feel your own spirit awaken, encouraged to expand, to take up the space you are meant to occupy. This work affirms a vital truth: our humanity, in all its messy glory, is holy.

As a deep feeler, thoughtful theologian, and brilliant writer, Callie Feyen navigates the intricate landscapes of parenting, identity, faith, and the seemingly ordinary moments in life. Her insights are poignant, causing you to catch your breath. Through her stories, we are gently reminded of who we are, who God is, and the essential practice of holding it all—the joy, the sorrow, the growth, the evolution—both lightly and with reverence.

You'll find, as I have, that Callie's unique lens will shape your faith and your story.

Xan Morgan
Director of Community Life
First Baptist Church
Ann Arbor, Michigan

Acknowledgments

Despite the fact that I begged my parents every weekend to change from Presbyterian to Catholic because the girls got to wear white, tulle-fluffed dresses when they got confirmed, I am grateful that I got to spend my growing up years at First Presbyterian Church of River Forest, Illinois. I didn't know that's where this book would begin, but I am grateful it did.

Thank you to those at First Presbyterian Church of Ann Arbor, Michigan, who encourage me regularly to write and to keep writing: Reverend Melissa Anne Rogers, Reverend Mark Mares, Reverend Jay Sanderford, Reverend Evans McGowan, Reverend David Prentice-Hyers, Reverend Hannah Lundberg, and Minister of Music & Fine Arts David VanderMeer.

While I can make no claim on the University of Notre Dame except that I taught step aerobics there, the place has made its claim on me. I spent many afternoons-turned-evenings in the Hammes Bookstore grading papers and planning lessons. The bookstore is where I met Tibby, Libby, Bridget, and Carmen of *Sisterhood of the Travelling Pants*. It is where I met Melinda Sordino of *Speak*. It's where I met a forgiven Judas. I was never a student there, but Notre Dame taught me daily about grace and faith, and to return again and again to story.

Thank you to Megan Willome, who spent an abundant amount of time on these essays while they were in manuscript form. Thank you for your keen, poetic eye. Thank you for helping me find and bring out the shimmer. Most of all, thank you for your friendship.

ACKNOWLEDGMENTS

To Hadley and Harper: from holding your hands as we make our way down three flights of stairs, to sitting in the passenger seat as you learned how to drive, every moment with you is enchanting. I love being your mama.

Finally, Jesse: whether we are sitting at Corby's in South Bend, figuring out the Metro in Washington, DC, or watching a soccer game, swim meet, or band concert in Ann Arbor, home is wherever you are.

1

When We Swung from Church Bells

FIVE OF US STAYED behind after Sunday School. We sat on top of the desks, and talked about the original *Star Wars* trilogy—isn't Jabba the Hut sick, and can you even believe Darth Vader was Luke's father?

Only whiffs of that morning's lesson were left: the smell of smoke from the candle our teacher always lit, a few Bibles left out, some crayons and pencils. We were studying Passover—not the Holy Week one, but the original, when you had to put blood from a goat or a lamb on your front door so God (or maybe it was an angel of God) would not kill that family's firstborn son. Pass. Over.

The lights were out in the classroom. I swung my feet, giddy from our conversation and also because I was talking to boys.

"Cookies should you get," Andrew told Jon, doing his best impression of Yoda and sending us into hysterics.

"Juice, too!" Maren said, giggling.

"You have to say it like Yoda," Jon teased.

"Too juice?" Maren attempted, and we all laughed harder.

↜

Church went like this each Sunday: 9:30–10:15 was Sunday school, 10:15–11:00 social hour, 11:00 to whenever the pastor stopped talking was the actual church service. (Unless it was football season; then church ended precisely at 11:45. Nobody in Chicagoland missed a Bears game.)

Too old to stand near our parents during social hour and too young to hang out in the youth group room, we lingered in our Sunday school room until it was just us that remained: Maren, Jon, Laura, Andrew, and me. We were in the in-between years, when we knew all about Moses, Esther, Mary, John the Baptist, and of course, Jesus, but we didn't have to declare anything just yet. We were at the door of the mystery, but hadn't opened it. We hadn't stepped in.

Eventually, we all would. We'd sit in our confirmation class, write our statements of faith, and present them to Session—our church elders. I remember the carpet in that room was red, and the table was thick and wooden and parts of it were engraved. It was not like the Sunday school rooms in the basement with the checkered linoleum floor and the foldable tables. Permanent things happened in that room.

I'd known these kids since we were 5 years old and singing, "I am a C! I am a C-H! I am a C-H-R-I-S-T-I-A-N!" and "Father Abraham, had seven sons" at the top of our lungs. We were at all the church potlucks, went to VBS, took turns being Mary and Joseph at each year's Christmas pageant until one year I insisted— begged, really—that I be Gabriel.

"Gabriel speaks!" I whined to Mrs. Pope, my Sunday School teacher, and yes, that is her real name. We told her once she was in the wrong denomination, but either she didn't get the joke or didn't think it was funny. Anyway, I wore her down and got the only speaking line in the entire pageant. I was the only kid who got to stand in the choir loft, shoot up, and startle Mary and the rest of the congregation with my, "BE YE NOT AFRAID!"

The evening of my debut I forgot my lines and muttered something like, "Hey Mary, don't be afraid, but you're pregnant," and promptly ran to the ladies' room, where I cried and cried.

Jon and Maren met me there. They must've been shepherds that year, and that's why they could sneak out. There's always so many shepherds.

They brought me cookies. Jon and Maren grabbed a bunch from the social hall and used them as an attempt to get me to come out of the bathroom.

"I can't slide them under the door, and I'm not coming in," Jon said, and I heard Maren gulp down a laugh, which made me laugh, and that's the extent of the memory. I don't remember either of them saying all would be well, or it wasn't that bad. I just remember they were there.

‽

Jon and Andrew came back with cookies and juice. Andrew handed me a sugar cookie with rainbow sprinkles—my favorite.

"There's a hole in the floor of the balcony," Jon said, brushing cookie crumbs off his khakis.

"So?" Andrew said, both taking the bait and baiting, as boys do.

"So I kind of want to know where it leads," Jon said.

Jon hadn't officially proposed the idea of heading to the balcony, lifting the piece of square that looks like the floor (to the uncurious eye or the eye that's focused on worshipping the Lord), and crawling inside to see what's there in the dark. We knew that's what he was getting at.

We drank the juice, hopped off the table, and went to find our parents to tell them the four of us would sit together during the service.

"Behave," is what my mom said.

Whether we behaved or not is up for interpretation. We answered the siren call of the hole and slipped ourselves into the dark while the Reverend said a thing or two about what it means to be a good Presbyterian.

What happened next is that we grew up. Off to high school, then college. We got jobs—teaching and business. Andrew owned a restaurant for a while. Maybe he still does. We lost parents and became parents. What I know of these friends now comes through the black-and-white overtures of social media.

There's no more crawling into the dark.

The church I attend these days is strikingly similar to the one I grew up in. Both are Presbyterian churches. Both are old, cathedral-like buildings with hundreds of nooks and crannies. I am almost fifty years old, with a husband and kids of my own, but I walk through the church's doors, and I still expect to see Jon, Laura, Maren, and Andrew again. It's not just reliving the stories I have of our church adventures. I also remember dipping parsley in salted water when our Sunday school class had a Maundy Thursday meal. I remember pouring grape juice into tiny cups with our dads the Saturday before Communion Sunday. We'd carry them into the sanctuary—our breath empty and quiet and somehow expectant—and the slight quiver of the cups as we placed them on the table were the only sounds heard.

I remember admitting to Laura and Maren I'd be out of my mind scared if I had been Mary, or that I didn't want God to call me to be a missionary. (In those days, it seemed that if one was "called" it was specifically and only to share God's love in another country without running water and electricity, and that was a real stretch for sixteen-year-old Callie.)

We held hands when we became Christians. "God, you know me," one of us said. "You know what I've done, and you know what I will do." We laughed at that part. I like to think God did too.

Once Laura and I were sailing her dad's boat on Lake Charlevoix, and we found ourselves heading for the strait that would lead us in Lake Michigan's deeper and rougher waters. We were having trouble turning around, and we were getting scared.

"Pray," Laura said. "We need to pray."

So I did. I prayed, and I think Laura prayed too, and I remember how close we were to the water and how Lake Michigan's blue lurked ahead. Lake Charlevoix's water was crystal and popped and snapped against the boat like it was warning us. I remember feeling like we were in a snow globe, except it was summer. What I mean is I got a sense of how small we were. I kept praying, and I was scared, but I was also calm, maybe even content. Some sort of resolution clung to me like the orange life vest I'd snapped on before we pushed off into the water.

⟵

There is an old lady at my current church. There are lots of them, but this one I tend to stay away from because she's a know-it-all, and I disagree with just about everything she says. During the social hour at church one summer morning, I watched with mild dread as she made her way to where I was standing, sure she was going to correct me for something I'd written or said lately.

"Your story," she began, wagging an index finger at me. "It reminded me of when I was a little girl."

She was referring to a story I'd shared about a time when Laura, Jon, Andrew, Maren, and I scaled the walls of our church during the ice cream social. I was sure this lady was about to tell me that when she was a little girl she ate her ice cream and then read her Bible and prayed, and that's what I should've been doing instead of inching my way along a six inch cement border, seven feet off the ground. I was bracing myself to hear that my dress was probably filthy—and my patent leather shoes, too—from my adventure, and what did my mother think of having to clean it all?

"We used to sneak up to the bell tower, my friends and I," she began, and she leaned in closer and cupped her hand to her mouth like she was going to tell me a secret.

"Your story reminded me of those days," she said, "when we swung from church bells."

She leaned away, clearly proud of herself as she relished my look of shock and admiration.

"Tell me more," I said, offering her one of my rainbow sprinkle cookies.

2

On Faith and Story

I HAVE A PROBLEM with Jesus' parables. I don't understand them, and He's always saying, "He who has ears, let him hear." I *do* have ears. I *am* listening. Jesus, I'm trying. But I don't get the story.

It reminds me of my high school French class. My teacher was in some kind of war—World War II maybe, I can't remember—but he rode his bike to school every day, which doesn't seem like a big deal except he rode something like two hundred fifty miles and not on one of those motorized bikes either. We would ask him how he biked in a suit and tie, and he told us he didn't. He folded his teaching clothes in such a way that when he pulled them out of the little knapsack he clipped to the back of his bike, they were crease-free. He learned how to do this because he was in a war.

"That is crazy," we would say.

"It's time to conjugate verbs," he would respond.

He had a poster on the wall of his classroom that read, "I know I'm somebody 'cuz God don't make no junk." I always chuckled at it. I liked the message, sure, but I liked it more for the grammatical irony: Here we were naming the 3,562 forms of a verb and "don't make no" is waving at us like a kid in the hallway trying to make us laugh.

One day he called on me to conjugate a verb. I want to say it was "essayer," my favorite verb because it means, "to try," but more likely it was something like "run" or "think." Anyway, I couldn't do it. I didn't understand how to change the verb, and I started to cry. My teacher moved so that he was just to the right of the poster, and he said nothing but he didn't let me off the hook either. I looked at the poster and then at him.

"I can't do it!" I yelled. "I don't get it!"

Nobody laughed. My teacher didn't yell back. All was silent.

I wiped my eyes and nose and picked up my pencil and pointed it at the paper while "God don't make no junk" pulsed between my ears.

Verbs drive me crazy. I need nouns. Give me something to hold. To feel. To eat. Of all the verbs the Bible uses to tell the works of Jesus, "eating" is the one I can get behind. I wonder if the eating leads to the preaching and the teaching and the healing and the forgiving and the calling.

A friend of mine has a daughter who, on a walk home from school recently, got into a heated argument with a kid who was using derogatory language. My friend's daughter told the kid to cut it out, but she wouldn't and so my friend's daughter—let's call her Esther—used the mother of all swears to tell the other girl to buzz off.

A third girl was there, let's call her Martha. Martha is not precious, but she's thoughtful and kind. She's the quiet one who makes sure everyone has sharpened number 2 pencils and who willingly and cheerfully packs extra Goldfish crackers to hand out to her friends. Using the mother of all swears in front of Martha is the equivalent of kicking a puppy.

Esther told her mom she knew Martha was upset and she wanted to apologize, but Esther was, after all, standing up for another human being. She was working for justice! Esther was upset that Martha didn't understand this, and so what do you do when you're changing from something elementary into something more nuanced? Can the friendship grow and stretch and become something new? Must we understand all of the story, or is it more important that we promise to keep listening?

Esther's mom suggested the two girls walk to a neighborhood coffee shop for hot chocolate because Esther's mom knows the settling power that cupping a warm mug of something frothy and bitter, sweet and soothing, has on two people grappling with growing up, friendship, and the usage of verbs.

I believe I was created and continue to be created wonderfully and fearfully by a God who's filled me with the stuff of stories—who calls me to figure them out enough to tell them. I believe confessing my doubt is vital to carrying out my faith. I believe God uses all that I am, all that I've done, all that I will become, and all I will do to point to His love for all of creation. I believe the Holy Spirit is a wild essence that dares us to use our imagination—to cling to it, especially in the dark, when murky monsters make their way to face us, hoping we have the courage to glimpse a new form and to bring it forth, walking and leaping and praising God.

3

Little Women, Innocent Birds

EVERY WOMAN I KNOW has a romantic story for the time they met and fell in love with *Little Women.* I am not one of them. My mom gave the book to me to read when I was at the age I suspect most girls are when they meet Jo and the gang, and maybe I gave the story a chance, but I doubt it.

I was not a reader growing up. My mom could've given me *Charlotte's Web* or *Bridge to Terabithia* or *Superfudge* or any book people my age wax poetic about reading, and I would've acted like she'd told me to stand behind a donkey, pinch its butt, and wait to see what happens.

Part of my attitude was my fault. I'm stubborn and rarely do anything I don't want to do. Another part came from what I learned about myself in school—I wasn't smart enough to read stories. Which extended to something even worse—I wasn't capable of bearing stories.

No one ever directly told me this, but just as St. Francis of Assisi told us to preach the gospel but only use words when we have to, I was shown year after year when standardized test scores came out that all my carefully penciled-in circles were proof I was below grade level. More proof showed up on my desk in the form of a thick stack of worksheets I'd have to complete—and complete perfectly—while my classmates read books and had book clubs, put on plays, and made colorful drawings of their favorite characters on giant pieces of posterboard.

However, I loved stories. I lived next door to a library, and before I was in school, I spent hours there, paging through picture books and making up a plot to go along with the pictures. I would check out so many storybooks the librarians would sometimes walk home with me, carrying part of the load. My mom and dad would read the books I brought home: *Hats for Sale, Blueberries for Sal, Miss Nelson Is Missing*. I loved them all. I tried to memorize them and read them to my baby dolls, as though I was a teacher.

But come kindergarten, reading became a problem to be solved, and I wasn't interested in solving it. So by the time my mom offered me *Little Women*, I don't know if it was my disdain for reading or my broken heart that kept me from giving it a chance. My mom kept trying—I think I understand now she wanted me to give myself a chance.

One morning I blew it, big time. I made the mistake of telling my mom I was bored, and she suggested I read a book. Eyes were rolled. There were huffs and puffs. Probably I stomped away. I wanted her to know that this was a stupid suggestion. I wanted a fight. I was baiting her.

"Fine," I said, slamming myself into a thick brown chair my dad sat in every morning to drink his coffee and read. I remember the legs of the chair creaked from the weight of my drama. "Let's see what stupid Jo and her stupid sisters are up to today," I said in some kind of sing-songy crazy librarian voice.

My mom took the bait. And the book. She never brought up *Little Women* again.

৻

More fiction. A year or two later I was at home, sick. Most likely I was faking it because there was a math or social studies test—or really any test—that day. My mom was working in a library in those days. She worked in the inter-library loan department, but I always thought what she did made her sound like a detective.

People would call her up or stop in the library and say that they were looking for a poem, or even a sentence or quotation from *The Chicago Tribune*, and my mom would find it for them. I don't know how she did it. What's more, she'd find additional articles and stories and poems for the patrons that would deepen whatever it was they thought they knew about what they were looking for in the first place. My mom has been thanked in the acknowledgements of several authors' books for helping them write their stories.

The day I was fake sick, my mom brought *To Kill A Mockingbird*, in VHS form, home from the library.

"Ew!" I complained. "It's black and white? How old is this? Why didn't you get me *Girls Just Want to Have Fun*"? (I was a true delight.)

"Would you just give it a chance?" I can still hear my mom's voice—strict and pleading, confident and questioning—as she said the words that would lead to one of my greatest and most mysterious pivots of all time.

Scout opened a box of treasures. Marbles rolled. A picture of a bird was torn down the middle of the paper. I was hooked.

The movie happened to me first, but the story imprinted itself on me in such a way that it made me willing to read the book. And willingness, I think, must've come from some belief that I *could* read it.

This is not the first instance of my mom helping me with a story using any means necessary. She used to write surveys for me on yellow legal pads so I could practice my name, address, phone number, and writing in complete sentences—all to help me endure the stress of taking tests. She found a recording of my favorite princess story, Cinderella, and I would follow along in my book. The "ding" from the record prompting me to turn the page was the equivalent to a pat on the back and a whisper to keep going; stay in the story.

I often had nightmares as a child and it was no use to tell me, "what you are afraid of is never going to happen." Instead, my mom would tell me to think about what else was true and good: ice cream and roller skating, donuts and trips to Lake Michigan when the waves were perfect for body surfing. Once I padded into her room late at night and stood at the foot of her bed and confessed that sometimes I get really angry at God.

"You can get mad at God," she said. "He can take it."

My mom gave me my first lessons in rewriting the narrative. She taught me about the disruptive grace that happens when we pass along stories, not knowing what will happen to us or to the ones we offer the stories to. We have no control over what a story will do.

Reading *To Kill a Mockingbird* didn't happen immediately after I watched the movie. In fact, I didn't read the book until I was an adult and teaching the book in an eighth-grade English class. (That I became a teacher is one of my life's great ironies.) But because I'd watched the movie a billion times, I was so comfortable with the story that I could bear it for my students. I thought of myself as a tour guide through a museum or amusement park.

Another thing happened: I noticed details that weren't in the movie when I read the book. Mrs. Dubose trying to harass the loneliness and fear out of herself. Calpurnia taking Jem and Scout to church. The pains Mayella Ewell took to grow red geraniums in slop jars. I was so comfortable with the foundation of the story that I felt good about paying attention to the details that made the book sing. I've read and taught *To Kill a Mockingbird* more than any book, and each time I find something new to think about, something new it offers, something new that makes me see the world differently, something new that changes me.

If I were to take a standardized test today, I would probably still be labeled "emergent" or "at-risk." Reading will always be difficult for me. As will faith.

My mom taught me that stories are thick, heavy doors waiting to be opened, inviting us to step inside and look around—no matter the dark and scary things we have to face—to see what shimmers. They are hoping we will stay, but if we don't, they will stay with us as a pinch in our side, a piece of dust in our eye, an ache in our heel. Waiting until we are disturbed enough to return.

4

Strange Grace

Here's a story about me and my friend Tim that I'm not sure I should tell. A friend's father had died, and Tim and I—along with our friends Chris and John—were heading to the funeral to pay our respects. On the walk to the service one of us had the where-withal to remember that probably it's a good thing to get a sympa-thy card, so we stopped at a drugstore.

It is no defense, but we were in eighth grade, and while we were all pretty okay kids, we did not have the maturity levels one needed for this task. The moment I walked inside the store, I made a beeline for the cosmetics aisle before stopping myself—in shock at my self-centeredness and lack of sensitivity—and pivoted to where the Hallmarks were. Tim was probably looking at baseball cards.

It was awkward, is what I'm trying to say. We weren't doing this right. We didn't know *how* to do this right. What fourteen year old would?

Eventually we found our way to the card aisle and stood there—awkwardly, in silence—until Tim started to laugh. Hard.

"These cards are all for old women!" he said, which sent me into a fit of giggles. Which, thanks to this brown-eyed, freckled boy I'd known since I was five years old, turned into hysterics.

I do not remember if we got a card. What I remember is how hard we were laughing and egging each other on, and of course it was wrong and inappropriate, but thanks to Tim, it was the lightest I'd felt during this inaugural navigation of death and grief.

I can't think about Tim and not think about baseball. My brother Geoff played on Tim's team for several years, and I spent many summer afternoons in the bleachers watching the boys play. I cannot see the White Sox logo without thinking of Tim. I believe the last time I saw him was on a summer night when I dropped him off at his house, and just as he'd gotten out of the car, John, who lived across the street, ran out of his house and threw a baseball at him. Tim dashed behind my car to catch the ball. I saw it in my rearview mirror. He was in mid-air—kind of like Michael Jordan except with a baseball—and he threw it back to John.

In fifth grade Tim gave me a Hershey bar on the playground of Longfellow School. For like three days he and I were "going out," and giving a girl chocolate was the probably thing to do. but probably what both of us really wished was to go back to the days when we walked home after school—a whole big group of us—making up some kind of game of tag or catch and laughing at our really stupid jokes.

Tim died before our senior year of high school. He was playing basketball with a bunch of our friends and got hit in the head. He was knocked unconscious and never woke up. I was in Tijuana, Mexico, on a youth group trip when it happened. By the time I came home, the wake, the funeral, all of it was over. I was left with details about a basketball game, and most likely I was too afraid to ask and not courageous enough to dwell on the tragedy of a childhood friend losing his life before his senior year of high school.

At the time I worked in our high school bookstore, and since I'd missed everything, my boss recommended that I see a counselor during my lunch breaks, and since I was a somewhat compliant kid and I adored my boss, I went.

I didn't know what to say, and this time there was no comedic relief to the awkwardness in the room. The counselor slid a piece of paper across the table and handed me a pen. "Maybe you'd like to write Tim a letter," she said, and then left me alone. It was the memory of Tim and I laughing in the drugstore that I wrote about.

I knew I wasn't going to send it to him, so I figured I might as well confess how I still got the giggles thinking about it. I told him I missed him. I told him I was sorry. But somehow, telling him this funny memory of the two of us felt truer—and sadder—than the other statements.

I think of Tim every June, and I get sad. It is true that he died way too young. It is also true that hearing Tim laugh was the sizzle of hot dogs on the grill. It was the glint of sparklers on July 4th. Maybe I shouldn't hang on to this moment, but if there is any redemption in it at all, it's that I remember, and in remembering I acknowledge how very complicated teenagers—and all of us—are. Tim showed me the strange grace that comes from all of who we are. He made me laugh. I am grateful to have lived on the same street as him for almost seventeen years. I am grateful he was my friend.

5

Monstrous Angels

A COLLAGE ESSAY ON TEACHING

1.

I GUESS IT STARTS with my mom's brown high heels. They were exquisite. Sleek and strong. They made a satisfying strike with each step I took on our hardwood floors. Granted, the shoes didn't fit, but they held the promise of fitting. And I could walk in them. When I did, I felt strong and sleek. And smart.

I didn't put them on every day, but some days, in that in-between time when it wasn't day but it wasn't evening either, I'd slip them on and walk around.

My parents set up a playroom in our basement. There was a ping-pong table, my brother's storm troopers and GI Joes (neither of which were a match for my Barbies), my dolls, and plenty of crayons and markers and paper.

I had an easel in the corner of the basement that was a chalk-board on one side, and on the other hung a slab of butcher paper. I would line up my dolls—I had enough for a class that would make a teacher demand an aide—and read stories to them.

On the days I would wear my mom's heels, I would walk slowly around my makeshift classroom, pointing to the pictures on the pages and asking my dolls, "What do you think will happen next?" Or, "Why is this person crying?"

I'd admit to my dolls that some of the words in the story were really tough for me to read. "Why don't we break the word down together?" I'd suggest, picking up a piece of chalk and carefully writing whatever complicated word I was struggling with on the board.

I was not conscious that I was giving myself what I wasn't getting in school. It did not occur to me that I was taking control of the situation by setting up a space where I was confident. None of that was deliberate. I was playing. I was pretending.

I was making myself believe.

2.

I am standing in front of twenty sixth-graders in a classroom in Detroit, Michigan. We are discussing *The Lightning Thief*. Percy Jackson has just learned he is a demigod, which means that all that he's been told about his weaknesses is wrong. His anger, his dyslexia, none of that actually needs to be fixed. They're gifts Percy needs to learn how to use.

"That's just like me," one student says. "I get so angry."

"Me too," another one says.

Percy also learns that he needs to find his father, the god Poseidon, but he doesn't have a clue where he is.

"That's me! That's me!" a student exclaims, and he is standing when he says it. "I don't know where my dad is, either!" He says this in the same tone one might shout, "Hallelujah! Praise the Lord!"

The classroom is silent, but I know we all feel a buzz in the room—a buzz with a stinger—waiting. This student who is standing up, proclaiming he doesn't know where his dad is, might not be happy about this fact of his life, but he's connected with Percy Jackson, the main character of the story. The hero.

"Okay, so," I begin, stepping toward him wearing my own high heels. These are flaming orange, like fire. "If Percy Jackson has been told all these alleged bad parts of him are actually good, do you think the stuff about us we've been told needs to be managed or fixed or even taken away could be used for good?"

I don't dare suggest that this boy can find his father. I don't think that's what he's hoping I'll confirm. I believe what he wants—what we all want—is something much tougher and more elusive to hold onto. "If Percy Jackson is the hero and you can relate to him," I say, taking one step closer, "what if you are a hero, too?"

3.

In a children's literature course we are discussing books with characters that we could relate to when we were kids. A handful mention Harry Potter and Hermione Granger. One mentions the *Big Nate* books, but then adds that while he thought they were funny, he always considered himself more reserved. His experiences didn't fit Nate's. "I wanted more than the punchline," he says.

"Yeah," another student adds, "I wish there were more books with shy people in them."

I have students create a character that they would've liked to read about when they were kids.

"It can be an animal, a fairy, a person," I tell them. "Whatever you want."

One person tells us about a princess whose superpower is hairstyling. Several of us want to meet this princess. Another student tells about a black cat who is sick and tired of its stereotype and wishes everyone would give her a chance to be whatever she wants to be.

One student talks about a monster that comes to school with a little girl. The little girl is shy, and that happens to be the monster's name. She wishes Shy wouldn't follow her to school. She doesn't like being shy, and she is afraid her monster will tell everyone.

Shy looks like a bean bag with arms and loves to give the little girl hugs. "You're good, you're good, you're good," Shy says as she gives the little girl a squeeze. The little girl learns she loves Shy. Soon, she tells her classmates about her monster. "Shy gives the best hugs," the little girl says. "Would you like one?" The little girl is so happy to share Shy with her classmates.

And her classmates are relieved because they have monsters, too. Loud, Messy, Scared, and Spacey. They didn't want their monsters coming to school with them either, but they did, and since the little girl shared Shy's hugs, her classmates shared what their monsters had too.

Messy had the best fingerpaints.

Loud was really funny.

Scared was superfast and also always knew the best hiding spots for hide-and-seek.

Spacey told amazing stories.

"So they're not bad monsters," I say.

"No," my student tells me. "They're good."

6

A Dangerous Belief

I ONCE TOLD MY husband, Jesse, that South Bend, the place where we were living, was a hole. I might've also used the word "armpit," but I'm not sure. It was a long time ago.

And so he showed me the library and the farmers' market. He took me to Macri's Bakery and bought us donuts, and we walked along the St. Joseph River to the salmon ladder, and he showed me where the water is too strong for them to swim, so people built this because the fish will always keep trying. They will always go against the current when the weather ripens the world for new growth. They will always swim upstream.

He took me to Molly McGuire's, a bar turned coffee shop because they'd gotten busted for serving minors. Bartenders became baristas, and pint glasses were filled with coffee. Sitting there felt like doing penance, but it wasn't redemptive. I sipped the coffee and felt a pull for what was.

He took me to the Hammes Bookstore, minutes after it was built at the University of Notre Dame. I'm not sure the cement on the surrounding sidewalk had dried. We wrote our wedding gift thank-you cards that first visit, and when my hand cramped, I walked around the store and looked at books.

The Hammes Bookstore is where I was introduced to a forgiven Judas. He was in a slim book, a devotional written from the perspective of those who had a part in Holy Week. Judas made no excuses for what he'd done, and yet here he was, fully loved and embraced, a sinner in the hands of an angry God.

How is this possible? Why not teach the salmon to swim the other way? Surely it'd make their lives easier. Why not switch out pint glasses for mugs and move on? Isn't it too painful and scary to believe that anything beautiful could grow from a mistake?

I was afraid of this new Judas, but I didn't want to let him go either. I know I didn't want to go back to the old Judas I had grown up believing in. I bought a class set of the books for my sixth-grade classroom. Back at school, we'd sit around the coffee table on an old couch and oversized pillows where we started every morning together, and we'd talk about Judas and Peter and Mary and Simon and Pontius Pilate and the mob and all of us who had a hand in this most horrifying story.

﹏

One morning, a mother came into my classroom and told me her son could not read this book.

"Judas is in hell," she told me. "He's in hell."

I did not argue with her. I said, "Okay," and I don't remember what happened after that.

Jesse tells me I'll always be okay as long as I can turn something into a story. He doesn't mean I live in a fantasy world (although at times he could mean that). He means that creating from the truth allows me to handle it.

The truth is both this mother and I were betrayed. She walked into my classroom and broke up what it was I was trying to create—what I had created—a place where a person believes that they have something good within them, no matter what they have done or will do. The truth is that something good can be worked and developed and offered as a gift to the world. The truth is I took her boy into a world she was protecting him from. I suggested to her son a dangerous belief—one much too wild to contain, one that cannot be ordered, one that breaks all order.

The truth is God shows up in old stories we think we know. God is beyond our joy and our doubt, our accomplishments and our failures, our good deeds and our sins. The truth is, God holds us in His hand in all of it.

The truth is God is never finished with us, even in death.

7

Wrestling Hope

It is the children's Bible, the one I've had since I was around seven, that I think of when I hear the story of God and Jacob wrestling.

I know the picture from my children's Bible well—both God and Jacob's muscles flexed, legs and arms intertwined. Jacob cowering and confused, but defending himself. God seems emotionless. The moon is full. They're battling on a mountain.

"Blessed are those whose help is the God of Jacob," Psalm 46 begins.

The God who Jacob cried out to for help? The God who hours later responds by starting a middle-of-the-night throw down? The God who made it so Jacob forever walked with a limp after they fought? How is that helpful? I'm not sure I want to be blessed if it means I have to wrestle with God.

The story follows me to a second-grade classroom during a Reader's Workshop. Today's question to guide students as they read is: what is a lesson a character learns that I can apply to my own life?

I think of Jacob and this line from his story: "Jacob fought back with all his strength . . . he knew that if he gave up, he would die."

I consider how terrified I'd be if I was grabbed in the middle of the night, or any time for that matter. What would I do? Would I fight back? Would I have the strength?

I look around the classroom. The whiteboards are now placeholders, no longer used for instruction, but rather for color-ful posters, calendars, and the day's "I can" statements, like "I can write many forms of poetry."

What if I can't, but I want to try anyway? What if I spend every day for the rest of my life writing, and it comes to nothing, save for finding the words to name what aches and what brings joy so that I can contend with it?

Once someone asked me how I knew God was calling me to write. I said I don't know, and moreover, I don't think God really cares if I write or not, but I know when I do, He is with me on the page.

He's with me in the struggle, that is. Once I've won the battle, once that essay, blog post, book, devotion is published, then the sun rises and He walks away. His back is turned, and I am vacant, exhausted, confused. I may not walk with a limp, but my steps are not steady. It is only when I pick my pen up again that He comes back. I write not because I feel called, but because I believe that if I give up, something inside me will die.

Hope and possibility feel like a lot like a wrestling match. I wonder if that's what being blessed is all about.

Come, Lord Jesus. Make it so we are all forever walking differently.

8

Wilderness Blooming

IN ONE OF THE schools where I work, a little girl—she can't be seven years old—kicks a teacher. She kicks a teacher and then runs to the library. That is my territory, where the stories are. It's not the territory of discipline. What do I do when a child, still pudgy from toddlerhood, carries so much anger and pain and fear that all her little body knows to do is kick it out?

I'm not interested in the disciplinary procedures I believe I must master first in order for me to hand off stories. I just want to hand off the stories. I want to give children stories so they can handle their own, so they can see the beauty and wonder in the make-up of their character, their plot lines, their conflicts. I want them to use stories to build their own arcs—colorful, miraculous, and filled with promise after a storm.

I don't care about anything else, but this child has hurt a teacher, and the teacher is standing in the doorway of the library, visibly hurt, and something needs to be done. I know the teacher doesn't want to be angry or in pain. I know this is not what she dreamed of when she signed her contract.

"Can you take her for a minute?" the teacher asks, and I nod, and the teacher closes the door.

It is just the girl and me now. We are standing on a giant, colorful carpet, and the sun shines heavy on us from the glass ceiling above, and I'm thinking one of us must make a move because I can't stand this heat. I inhale to suggest a story, but she bolts from the sunlight and screams, "I'm not reading no story!"

I want to leave the light too, but I stand still because I don't want her to think I'm chasing her. I won't chase her. I won't keep her here.

If she would stay, I would show her the book *Bloom*, about a fairy who was told to leave the kingdom because she made such a mess of things. But what the king hadn't realized, or didn't want to acknowledge, was that the magic could only happen if a mess happened first.

The little girl and I—we would sit on the comfy couch or the beanbag chairs or at a table if she likes, and she would read to me, or I'd read to her, or we'd take turns, each reading a page. We would draw pictures of the fairy and the kingdom. I wonder if she'd like that. I have brand-new crayons, and they're triangular shaped— I guess those are easier to hold than the circular ones, the edges more sturdy. I would offer her those.

Maybe we'd talk about the messes we've made. Like the time I said "butt" in first grade and had to come in at recess and write a note to my mom and dad about swearing. Or the time I ran to my fifth-grade teacher, breathless from anticipation, because we'd taken a math test, long division—the devil's math—and I'd studied and studied, and I knew I'd done well. I knew I'd get a sticker. I asked her how I did, and she looked at me and broke into laughter so beastly I forgot she was my teacher. "Awful," she told me. "You did awful."

Later something sad would happen to her. Not tragic, but sad, and she would tell our class about it, and she would start to cry, and I would return that beastly laugh, and not for a second feeling sorry for her.

We could share with each other these messes we've made while we drew pictures of castles and fairy wings, while we dreamed up a kingdom where messes are usable.

Instead we face each other, motionless, each of us trying to figure out how to bloom.

9

Hopeful Red Geraniums

MY FAVORITE PART IN *To Kill a Mockingbird* happens in chapter seventeen, when Scout gives readers a picture of the Ewell residence: "the plot of ground around the cabin look[ed] like the playhouse of an insane child," she tells us. It's a dreary paragraph with a grocery list of descriptions that support Scout's observation. I'm not of the haunted house type, but if I were, this paragraph would be what I would base my inspiration around.

My favorite part comes next, when Scout tells us about a corner of the Ewell yard that baffled Maycomb because in that corner sat "six chipped-enamel slop jars holding brilliant red geraniums." Word on the street is they were Mayella Ewell's. Mayella Ewell, who has never seen kindness in her life, never been treated with love and respect. Mayella Ewell, who has no friends, and who had to drop out of school after a year or two to work. Mayella Ewell, who snapped the mockingbird's wings. She's the one who cleaned out the old slop jars, went to the hardware store or the farmer's market to buy the seeds for the red geraniums. She's the one who learned how much water to give them so they'd grow, and where to put those jars so they'd face the sun. She's the one who had to trudge through that nasty yard, kneel down next to those flowers and look to see if anything was growing.

What do we do with this kind of beauty? It certainly complicates things. It's hard for me to hate Mayella Ewell for one thing.

This scene makes me look at evil for a long time until I can find something good to fix my eyes on, even if it's a remnant of what was, or what could've been. This scene reminds me that people are not always who they seem to be. Sometimes they can't show another side. Sometimes they don't know that there is another side to show.

This is the part my eighth-graders and I are studying in class. They are working on a little project I call, "Slop Jar Beauty." They need to create a scrapbook of six memories: three from *To Kill a Mockingbird* and three from their own lives. Each memory they write about and draw must show something dark (fear, sadness, anger), but the students need to find what shimmers in each memory as well. Last year when I tried this project, one student wrote about why mangoes are his favorite fruit; it was the last meal he had with his grandmother before she died. Another wrote about being sad he and his family had to move, but his parents let him have a say in the house they'd pick next. He chose one with a red door because it was his favorite color. Another found beauty in the leftover pedals that were sent to Jem from Mrs. Dubose. *Don't forget you lost your temper, Mr. Jem,* this student wrote. *Don't forget you read to me every day for a month so that I could die peacefully.*

This project was easy to present to last year's eighth-graders. They were risk takers. I shine when I have a class like this, and I cower when I don't. "I'm as good as you'll let me be," I used to say in my early days of teaching. I've been thinking a lot about that statement now that I have this year's eighth-graders, and I think I have it wrong. Why should I be as good as someone will let me be? Where's the grace in that? Why should I hold back something that could change the way they see themselves or the world just because I have a group that acts like the Herdmanns?

I don't do it to punish them. I second guess myself because I'm afraid. They snicker. They roll their eyes. They're going to say this project is dumb, I think, so instead I should just give them a test: Who defended Tom Robinson? Who plants red geraniums in her front yard? What was Scout for the Halloween play? Pick a theme for the story and in three paragraphs explain it.

If Mayella can grow something beautiful in her world, then I can do the same in mine. She is an example of someone who had a mustard seed of faith to hope for something to take care of and make beautiful. I don't believe she knew whether those flowers would bloom. My guess is she scrubbed those chipped slop jars in an act of misery and desperation and loneliness. I imagine her crying as she cleaned. I imagine that, despite how awful her life was, the idea of creating something, of attending to it, no matter what the outcome would be, was enough to fill those jars with a bit of soil, press a few seeds into it and give those seeds a drink of water.

The day I presented my "Slop Jar Beauty" project, three students were non-stop snickering and talking. I stopped what I was doing, walked over to them and told them this story:

> "When I was in eighth grade, I was supposed to read *Animal Farm*. I had no intention of reading that book. I wasn't into reading, and I really wasn't into animals who could talk.
>
> I came to class during that unit unprepared and ready to mess around with my friends instead of participating. I remember once I tied a kid's sleeves to his desk chair so that when the bell rang he wouldn't be able to leave class.
>
> One day my teacher took my desk and chair out in the hallway and told me to sit there for the remainder of class. I did, staring at the cover of *Animal Farm*, and about 15 to 20 minutes later he stepped out of the classroom and placed an index card on my desk. On the card he wrote that while it may not seem like it now, he cares about me and believes I am better than the way I am acting. He wrote that he hopes I'll make better decisions from now on.
>
> The nerve of that guy, I thought, thinking I was better than this. I'm not better than this, and I'm not reading this stupid book.
>
> I didn't read *Animal Farm*, but I kept that card. It was on my bulletin board in my room next to pictures of my friends, song lyrics, and movie ticket stubs. I took it to college with me.

I can't make you read *To Kill a Mockingbird*, and I certainly can't make you like the story. I don't know if I would've liked the story in eighth grade either. But I do think you are better than the way you are acting. I do believe there is something inside of you that is waiting to come out, and it might not be this book that brings it out, but the reason you come here Monday through Friday is to look for what's inside you, and to fight to bring it out. Right now though, you are not ready to be in this classroom. So I'm going to ask you to leave.

I want you to go upstairs with a piece of paper and sit in the administrator's office. You are to summarize what I said, and tell me three things you will do to change so that you can come back and figure out what it is that is inside of you because I think there's more than what you're showing right now."

I shook while I spoke. I cried on the way home from school. I was nauseous the rest of the day. I worried I got it all wrong. After all, those red geraniums were showing off their brilliance in the Alabama sun when Mayella took advantage of Tom Robinson. Then she went to court and lied about it, and poor Tom Robinson died. Those geraniums weren't enough to soothe her tortured soul.

Several years ago I went back to my eighth-grade English teacher's classroom after I was a teacher. I showed him the index card he placed on my desk. I thought he'd be happy to see I still had it, and to see what I've done with my life, but he flinched as though he was shaking the memory off of himself. I didn't understand why until last week, and now I wonder what kind of toll this digging around in the dirt and hoping for things unseen takes on people.

I've always thought that the reason I love this scene in *To Kill a Mockingbird* is because it is proof beauty grows everywhere, no matter what we do or who we are. I've always looked at it as a religious metaphor: Jesus seeps through it all, and there's nothing we can do to stop Him. Now though, I think what I mean is contained in this scene haunts me: I try to grow things, I try to create stories, I try to teach because I will die if I stop grasping for and imagining beauty. I'm wondering now whether Mayella even noticed how brilliant her red geraniums were. My guess is she'd be embarrassed and maybe even flinch in disgust if someone were to tell her how beautiful they are.

Maybe all we get is the opportunity to work with seeds before they're beautiful, and hoping for things unseen is plenty.

10

Fake Prayer

"BUT DEAR GOD PLEASE give me some place, no matter how small, but let me know it and keep it," Flannery O'Connor writes in her journal[1]. "If I am the one to wash the second step every day, let me know it and let me wash it and let my heart overflow with love washing it."

What a comfort, I think, to know what it is I'm supposed to do. To have God literally come to my front door and hand me a broom.

"Sweeping?" I'd say, holding the door open for Him. "Great. I'm on it. How about some coffee, first?"

He'd leave the broom on our front stoop and come in.

I'd tell him how relieved I am to know sweeping is all I'd have to do from now on. We'd sit across from each other, cupping our mugs that rested on the table Jesse built for me—a present for earning my MFA.

"I mean, I love to write," I'd confess, "but good Lord, I hate what comes after."

He'd nod, maybe take a sip of His coffee.

"The promoting, worrying about the reviews on Amazon, trying to explain what the book is about or what my platform is. God, I don't even know what my books are about. Do you know?"

I think there'd be silence after that.

1. O'Connor, *Prayer Journal*, 38.

So I'd say, "That's why I'm so glad you gave me this broom, so I don't have to worry about this shit anymore. Oh, sorry. I probably shouldn't swear in front of you. But God, You knew I thought it anyway, so what's the difference? Besides, didn't You make the word up in the first place?"

"And anyway, I just need to focus on my sweeping now. No more social media and comparing myself to what everyone else is doing. No more asking bookstores if I can please come to their store to read my book. I don't even want to go to AWP—like, ever."

I'd stand up and walk to the kitchen to get the coffee pot and refill our mugs.

"I bet Flannery O'Connor didn't have to worry about AWP. Or hashtags."

At this point, I think God would complement my coffee (because I make excellent coffee). "Well, maybe I could make coffee for people after I swept the stairs," I'd say.

"God, I'm talking your ear off, aren't I?"

There'd be silence, maybe a whiff of wind against the window. Maybe a cardinal landing on a tree branch outside.

"Do you know *The True Story of the Three Little Pigs*, where the wolf proclaims he's innocent? That he actually had a cold and the only reason he was at the pigs' house was because he needed some sugar to bake a cake for his grandma? It was his sneezing that blew the houses down."

"I read that story to a couple of classes recently and one boy, I know you know which one, stood up from the carpet at the end where the wolf is in jail, asking for sugar, and with his fists clenched he shouted, 'He's innocent! He's innocent! He shouldn't be in prison!'"

"I know you know his mom's situation, Lord. All I could do was close the book so he wouldn't see the wolf behind bars and tell him that I agreed—the wolf is innocent."

"We read a poem about spring the other day, this boy's class and I. He was in a grumpy mood when he walked into the library, banging lockers with his fists and feet and scowling. I've known this boy for two-and-a-half years. He's always been boisterous and rambunctious, but not like this. It's hard to see him like this, but we read the poem, and I said we were going outside to hunt for spring because that's what you have to do in Michigan—hunt for that green growth."

"He stood up again, smiling this time: 'I remember! I remember when we did that with you last year! And we looked for buds, and we found grass and heard birds.' He stopped and looked at the ceiling, still smiling. 'And the sun was shining,' he ended, making eye contact with me. He remembered correctly. The day was frigid, but the sun was out, and it felt so good, so we stayed outside longer than we probably should've."

"I'm not saying I did anything for this kid. Except it was nice to see him smile and remember spring, and when he talked about the wolf, it was good to pay witness to as much of himself as he could let out. I hope letting it out helped him, or will help him as he grows. I hope the innocence of the wolf will stay with him."

"Earlier this week another little boy pulled on my dress, asking me if he could please get a book from the return bin. I told him yes, and he dug up a thick book of fairy tales. He held the book like he was hugging it. 'Thank you, Mrs. Feyen,' this kindergartener said, as if I'd let him have recess all day for the rest of the school year. 'Mrs. D. reads us all our stories, and she didn't get to this one yet.'"

"'I do,' Mrs. D told me. 'I read every single book.'"

"The little boy smiled and nodded and then went to find a spot to read, while his teacher and I watched him."

"'He's gonna get himself out of whatever bad situation he's in,' Mrs. D said to me. 'He's gonna make it.'"

"She didn't say it like she'd hoped this was true. The way she said it, it had already happened. It was a fact. This boy reading fairy tales about wolves and dragons and poison apples is going to be OK."

Something tells me God wouldn't have all that much to say during this visit. Maybe He brought the broom over so I'd let Him in and not because He really thought I'd use it. Like I'd ever sweep. I think the last time I did, I was seven and pretending to be Cinderella.

I bet Flannery O'Connor didn't really mean what she wrote about a small place when she was praying. Maybe she was wrestling with *Wise Blood* or *The Violent Bear It Away* and wondering what the point of writing even was. Maybe she was considering what the point of a story is in the first place.

I bet that's when she asked for a broom, and I bet that's when God showed up with one. I bet she left it in the yard with the peacocks and the two of them went inside. I bet she offered Him something stronger than coffee. She'd get to talking, and I bet without realizing it she'd start to tell Him a story or three about what she observes in this world that's beautiful and horrifying and usually it's both at the same time and she doesn't know what to do with this kind of disorder except to write it down and share it with others so she doesn't have to bear it all by herself.

I bet she never picked up that broom.

11

Fearfully and Wonderfully Made

I AM FACING A mirror in a clothing boutique, and I am not pleased with what I see. It is my habit to allow the clothes I wear to guide how I feel and think about myself, and my favorite pieces are those that serve many moods and offer multiple looks.

But the dress doesn't fit, not even in the largest size. I am devastated. I scrutinize myself from top to bottom—my graying, stringy hair, the bags under my eyes—when another customer walks in, and I hear the saleswoman greet her, both their voices light and breezy, with that affected teenage girl tone. I can't ever understand why such beauty—that tone, this dress—can carry such a sting.

Madison Beer croons lusciously overhead. I have one of her songs on my running playlist—something about the evils of social media. It's catchy, but I don't understand, or I don't want to understand what she's singing about. I'm not her target audience.

This place is not for me, I realize as I very, very carefully shimmy out of the dress while ignoring the image in the mirror that resembles something of an overstuffed potato sack.

I walked into this boutique hoping for something to show me I am strong and beautiful, but maybe it is my larger and softer parts that now need to be exposed. Maybe it is what's been labeled as weak, as less than, that now shows the mystery and grace of being wonderfully and fearfully created.

I step into my well-worn jeans and pull my T-shirt over my head and look at myself again. Somewhat resolved, I pull the curtain to the dressing room back and walk out.

"Did you find the right size?" the saleslady asks me.

"No," I say. "Everything was too small."

I walk out of the boutique believing a new thing is being created within me.

It's just too large for this store.

12

Magnification

A FRIEND OF MINE recently asked me if I ever wondered whether Mary had postpartum depression.

"Or did God give her a pass on that?"

I laughed and responded that I don't think God gave Mary a pass on anything. She faced all of it: a crazy Gabriel busting in on her and delivering news that seemed scientifically impossible and not at all romantic, giving birth in a barn, her teenaged son ditching her to talk with the church folk and leaving Mary in a panic, the slow and terrifying realization that the way in which her son would save the world would mean to be brutally beaten and die.

But she's in the first chapter of Luke, telling us that her soul magnifies the Lord, and I am thinking of my fifth-grade science teacher, who showed us how to carefully peel the skin of an onion and clip it on glass, then adjust the knob of our microscope so we could see all the intricate designs of each layer. We rolled our eyes before we looked. We wanted to dissect frogs and cows' eyes! We didn't even eat our vegetables, so why would we want to look at them? Our teacher, Ms. Gardner (I kid you not), rolled her eyes right back and told us to look, and we wanted recess, and she was a much better eye-roller, so we did what she said.

We were quiet after that, save for our steady breathing and the scratch of our pencils on paper as we tried to capture what had been magnified.

If God gave Mary a pass what would that mean for the rest of us? What would that mean for all we've been called to hold, to create, to welcome into our lives? I don't think Mary was sugarcoating her situation when she sang her song of praise. I think Mary offered a vulnerable submission for Immanuel.

O come, O come, Immanuel. Do not give us a pass. Give our souls the work of magnification.

13

Witness

noun: evidence; proof.
verb: give or serve as testimony.

My nouns are:
Cheerios on the floor
toy trucks and dinosaurs, too
tulle skirts and stickers
sippy cups filled with apple juice

my verbs are:
going to the park
walking to the library
eating ice cream with rainbow sprinkles
wiping little hands and mouths from the treat's stickiness

My confessions:
sometimes I want more nouns and verbs
not different ones, just more
do I have more proof to give?
More ways to serve?
I don't think I want
to be like Mary
treasuring and pondering

it all up in her heart
but saying nothing.
I want my heart
to beat differently

14

Reading The Bible
with My Four-Year-Old

First, I start with poetry. This morning's poem is "Not Like A Dove"[1] by Mary F. C. Pratt, and she describes the Holy Spirit as something scary, something that "take[s] our treasures" for its "glittering hoard," and I consider that perhaps our treasures are nothing unless the Holy Spirit has a hold of them—her claws around what I think is mine.

I like this poem. I like that it doesn't describe the Holy Spirit as peaceful or comforting. Instead, it's powerful, dangerous, even assaulting.

My daughter, Hadley, is sitting across from me, and her eyes are almost glaring at me. Waiting? Wondering? Lost in thought? I look at her for a moment and pick up my coffee mug. Before I take a sip, I ask, "What's next?"

She scoots off her chair taking her juice with her in one fluid moment. "I'm gonna drink my juice and sit on your lap."

But I want to sit and think about this poem. Why is the Holy Spirit described as a dangerous predator that comes unexpectedly into our lives, taking all that we treasure? Why does the poet invite the Holy Spirit to do that?

---

1. Pratt, "Not Like a Dove."

Why, in this moment sitting with my coffee cup, journal, Bible, this poem, all of it open, all of it ready for me, is it more important than my child sitting on my lap, her hair tangling up with mine as she squeezes herself into me, as though she's trying to re-enter my womb?

15

Making Believe with Jesus

I AM SITTING IN our sunroom reading a magazine when Hadley asks me if it's okay to make up stories about Jesus. She is supposed to be napping. Every afternoon, for two glorious hours, this is what is supposed to happen. Hadley has other plans.

"What do you mean?" I ask her, and she takes my hand and leads me to the nativity scene on our coffee table. The wooden figures—the cows, the shepherds, the kings, Mary and Joseph—are all lying down.

"All these people and animals are dead," Hadley tells me, watching my reaction carefully.

"Oh dear," I say.

"But then, God touched Every. Single. One," she tells me this as she lifts Baby Jesus and gently swipes each figure with him. "And then they lived."

"That's a good story," I tell Hadley.

"There's more, Mama," Hadley says and goes on to tell me that everyone went out to dinner and then got married. "Wait. They got married first, and then they went out to dinner," Hadley says, reinforcing that this next part—the living part—is just beginning, and it might be more hard to understand than the first part.

A few days later I have my youngest daughter, Harper, on my hip while I'm chasing Hadley around our apartment in an attempt to get her ready for preschool. Our mornings aren't stressful, but they are also not calm, and this morning I'm in a bad mood. Dishes are everywhere, the garbage is overflowing, and somehow the girls have taken out every toy they own and flung them all over the floor. I don't like these days, when everything is out of order, when I can't keep up, when I am snippy and my words to Hadley and Harper are harsh. Feeling defeated but knowing there's no such thing as defeat in motherhood, I take a deep breath—about my only form of prayer these days—and grab the garbage and hustle the girls out the door.

We live on the third floor of this building, and it's a quest getting outside with a three- and one-year-old. Today Hadley wants to get downstairs without touching a single step. Harper, who hasn't mastered walking, wants to go downstairs without help. "Do it self," she says, swatting at my hand. Their passion to literally do the thing they can't breaks my heart and also makes me angry. Why do I have to be the one to explain to them the impossibility of their dreams, that we could all end up in the ER if I let them try?

This is how it goes for me these days. The enormity of my emotions paired with the necessary tasks like walking down the stairs sends me to worst-case scenarios because I see all that can go wrong. Nothing is simple anymore.

It is the garbage truck that saves us. Hadley and Harper are both in awe of and terrified of garbage trucks. No matter what they're doing, they will run to our window and watch the loud and mysterious ritual of throwing things away. We hear its beep and clank as it moves to where our dumpsters are. The three of us stop our ruminating and whining and pleas to do things without help, and we all freeze.

"Girls," I whisper, "I think if we work together we can see the garbage truck up close!"

They gasp. Hadley holds onto the railing and lifts a foot. I grab Harper's hand. She lets me.

"You want to try to get close?"

"Yes!" they shout, and we make our way outside.

We make it in time to see the truck beginning to pull away, its murky green body slides past us like some enchanted thing.

The man driving the truck sees the three of us holding hands and staring and stops the truck.

"One more!" he yells out to the back of the truck, where another man hops off and starts walking toward us.

I've forgotten I'm holding garbage, and remembering that, I feel a jolt of shame. Are there recyclables in this bag that I was too lazy to sort out? What about compost starts? The man waves his hand for me to give him my bag, but I am frozen by all my "should haves" and "should bes." I should have woken up earlier to take care of these chores before taking care of the girls. I should be more organized. I should be more calm.

All this from a sack of garbage.

The man sees that I'm not moving, so he steps off the truck and walks toward me, opening his hand. I step off the curb and lift the bag. The truck breathes smoke and rumbles as the man leans in and takes my bag.

"Have a good day," he says and walks back to the truck.

"Thank you," I say.

I turn toward my girls, rubbing my hand where the handles of the bag made a mark from its weight. We watch the truck move on—its beeping a steady ring, almost like church bells.

We stand there until its smoke—like windfall—swirls into the air and out of sight, and not knowing anything else to do, we walk into the rest of our day.

16

Stories Help My Unbelief

I WAS NEW TO blogging when I met another blogger, who I will call Bernice, for coffee one afternoon in Washington, DC. We met because we both loved and wrote about children's literature, although she analyzed the books—how they work, what was important about them and why—while I wrote about what Hadley, Harper, and I did with the books (crafts and activities), and how they reacted to the stories.

"You have to know precisely what you're writing about," she began. "Your first post should be all about what you will explore on your blog." Bernice ripped a packet of sugar in half, and sprinkled it onto the foam milk heart. "Then you have a 'start here' button that links to that post." She swirled the sugar and the heart with a metal spoon that clanked against the mug.

"Have a content calendar," Bernice said. "Create a call to action. Don't forget freebies!"

I thought we were going to discuss *Frog and Toad* or *Pinkalicious*. I wanted to ask her what she thought of *Pete the Cat* or *What Happens on Wednesdays*. I didn't know I was getting a lesson in Blogging 101.

I present as nice, so I made like I was interested in Bernice's lecture, but I was disappointed. I didn't have a call to action. I wouldn't know what to call readers to do except read. My content calendar was a small notebook I kept in my diaper bag and scribbled in from time to time. When I had more time, I'd open it and choose an idea to expand upon. I had no clue what my blog was about. I've now been blogging for 20 years, and I still can't say what I write about.

"Do you know what a blog roll is?" Bernice asked me.

I wasn't sure if a "yes" or a "no" would make her stop talking about the layout of a blog. If I said, "yes," would she make me tell her what it is? And if I said, "no" would she flip her laptop open and show me five thousand examples, annotating the merits of each?

I didn't answer quickly enough, so she opened her computer and showed me her blog roll. What seemed like a grocery list for someone who's never eaten before spread out before me. "How do you even read all these?" I asked Bernice.

"It's networking," she said. "It's good to support each other. That reminds me," Bernice added, "You really need to participate in blog hops."

Just as I was about to scream and put an end to this friendship that never was, the name Severus Snape caught my eye.

"Snape!" I said.

"What?" Bernice said.

"Severus Snape! Right there! On your blog roll!" I pointed to her blog roll like I was in grade school, identifying the parts of speech.

"Oh," Bernice said. "Right."

"I LOVE Snape," I said, like he was an old friend. "I always knew he was good."

Bernice laughed through her nose. "No, you didn't," she said, and shut her computer.

Our friendship did not bloom; however, my love for Snape did. Maybe Bernice was right—I didn't always know Snape was good. I always hoped he was, though. I wanted to believe that the brooding and the tortured souls, the stubborn and the sly, were capable of doing good. The more I got to know Snape, the more I rooted for him (and consequently, the less enchanted I was with Sirius Black). I wouldn't have minded Snape as a teacher. I liked the gruff, the blunt, the strict. I really liked the dark.

A couple years later my wish was granted when my second year mentor in graduate school was Lauren Winner. Am I comparing Lauren Winner to Severus Snape? Yes. Does she know this? No.

I often heard the phrase "I've found my people" from my classmates while I was in graduate school. That was not true for me. I do not suffer imposter syndrome, but I carry with me years of being told that I'm remedial, that I need enrichment skills, that I am not smart enough to be in class with the academically advanced. This was (part of) the luggage I carried with me to Santa Fe and Whidbey Island where the MFA residencies took place. I could read and write, but I wrote about Hadley and Harper. I read children's literature and young adult novels. I did not get Emily Dickinson and Gerard Manley Hopkins. Flannery O'Connor scared me to death, and I didn't understand why Cormac McCarthy refused to use quotation marks.

The people who I went to school with seemed established: profs and pastors, filmmakers and doctors. I was a stay-at-home-mom. I feared every inch of me screamed "Mommy Blogger."

But writing motherhood was an opportunity for me to attend to and contend with my days and consequently, with my faith. I'd heard blogging wasn't really writing. I understood that clicking the "publish" button on my Blogspot account didn't equate to capital-P publishing. I was well aware of the stereotype that swirled around me, threatening to seep its way into my soul.

However, something settled within me when I wrote. I believed I was offering up something I created, and in that sense, I believed I was praying.

"Here's what you gave me," I told God, "and here's what I did with it." It never occurred to me not to believe I wasn't really a writer. I had no time for that doubt.

Maybe it is make-believe, but when I wrote motherhood, I often thought I was doing what Mary couldn't do. I believe she treasured a whole lot in her heart, but I also wonder whether the writer of that phrase meant it as a directive to moms: treasure these moments. Don't wonder. Don't question. Don't speak.

I wanted—and continue to want—to speak.

I believed Lauren would push me beyond what I thought I could do, but I was also scared of that pushing. Imagining her as Snape helped me make a story from the intimidation and struggle I was experiencing.

We met one-on-one in the beginning of the semester, and Lauren asked me to come with a list of books I'd recently read. I flinched as I passed my collection of picture books, early readers, and young adult fiction across the table toward her. I expected her to ask me just what I thought I was doing here, but instead she suggested a handful of young adult novels to read as I studied Creative Nonfiction.

I thought she was giving me an out, or dumbing down the requirements because she knew how difficult all of this was for me. All this reading. All this writing. All this dealing with leaving my children and flying across the country to chase a dream that did and will always eternally break my heart.

"Pay attention to what the mothers are doing in the stories," she told me before our meeting ended.

In one story a mother hops from one creative burst of an idea to another, one of which is a restaurant where customers grind their own meat. Her husband and daughter laugh at her ideas and efforts. They get annoyed too. The mom's pursuits are funny, but at times they're ridiculous and embarrassing. While I was captivated by the teenage girl, lovesick and figuring herself out, I was also cautiously intrigued by her mother and her frazzled strength, making a place for herself in a life that is hers but that—at times—she feels lost in.

I kept reading and watching out for the mothers. How did they act? What did they say? What were they interested in? I was learning how books worked, yes, but I was also learning that while the mother might not be the main character of the story, she is still in the story.

Lauren was gruff and blunt. She did not suffer this fool, and she was one of the only teachers I've had who treated me like I was capable of doing the work. I've come to think of her as a doctor of stories—prescribing books and poetry to help the development of human beings.

And I see now that Lauren wasn't handing me a way out when she suggested I read young adult literature. She handed me a way in.

17

Hail, Mary

It is hot at the soccer game and Harper's playing goalie, and I'm not sure which is stressing me out more. I should be used to this—the slow fluctuation of the transition into fall and watching my kids defend a ball. Every year, though, it is difficult. Fall arrives on its own sweet time, no matter my impatience, and my girls try, and try, and try again. It's not that I don't have time for it—the transition and the trying. (Does it matter if I don't? Everything's always changing, and being alive means we try.) It's that it is hard to watch.

The wasps become more aggressive because they know their days are numbered. Some leaves change too quickly and turn brown and crusty before they turn brilliant. The girls rush out onto the field hopeful and uncertain at the same time, and I watch with the same perspective.

I sit in my foldable chair in-between other moms, and I wonder about Mary. I think of her at thirteen, seeing Gabriel. I think of her feeding her son, knowing what he'll have to do someday. I think of her treasuring moments in her heart. If she could do all that, surely I can watch my whimsical, lanky girl play soccer.

I watch Harper as the ball gets closer. I remember a mother telling me once that if the goalie misses, that might be the final mistake, but it wasn't the only mistake. Harper's teammates seem to understand this because they are fighting and staying with the ball, and Harper's bouncing on her toes, ready, but I hope she is also watching these girls work to ensure that she doesn't have to be the one to make the final mistake. This feels like a form of friendship, this watching out for each other, and I am thankful for it.

"Does anyone have ibuprofen?" the mom to my right asks. Her older daughter isn't feeling well. The mom to my left has some and passes it over.

A girl who looks bigger and stronger prepares to kick the ball in the goal. Harper raises both hands in the air and lowers them down, slowly, like the ball is some kind of fantastical, magical entity she can control. She barely touches the ball, but it is hers. She picks it up and throws it away.

I want to laugh at this child who does everything on her own time. Who, when she was in kindergarten and learning to write, cried because she couldn't make the stem of the letter P as long as she pleased. Who, upon hearing the words "no" or "don't" would throw a fit, but do it anyway. Who feels sorry for Voldemort. Who saves soccer balls in slow motion.

"She looks like a queen," one of my friends says, and the laugh I've been holding in comes out. That's exactly what she looks like, and I laugh louder, thankful to have moms to watch this game with, thankful we share in watching our changing children try.

There is a sacredness to these sideline conversations. We always laugh—at ourselves, and our kids—but the laughing brings forth other remarks and comments. One mother asks if any one of us could drive her daughter home from school one day next week. (Yes, always yes. We will figure it out together.) We talk about the business of September and whose kid already has been sick.

"I was so sick last February," I say. "And Jesse was out of town." I uncross my legs and wince in disgust at the sweat marks on my pants. "I wasn't sure how I was going to get the girls to school."

"Well," the mom who has the ibuprofen says, "now you know me."

She is the same person who, when I told her I was running home from our girls' soccer game last spring, and it would be my longest run yet, and I didn't think I could do it, said without any hesitation: "here's what you'll do: you'll run when you can run, and if you need to walk, you'll walk. Either way, you're going home."

I wish there was something in the Bible about Mary's friends—how about an entire chapter? Did Jesus play soccer? I wish Mary hadn't treasured all of it in her heart. I wish the verse went something like this: "And Mary treasured all these things in her heart until she found friends who'd meet her for a drink and she could laugh and maybe cry until her belly ached and then go back to being the mother of the Son of God."

Because you'd have to have some friends for that role.

↫

Next Saturday it is at least twenty degrees cooler, and another friend and I are on the sidelines discussing the Harry Potter books while we watch the girls play. I tell her my favorite line in the series comes from Molly Weasley in the seventh book. She's fighting Bellatrix, and the two of them are having such a duel that even Voldemort and Harry Potter stop in awe. "Not my daughter, you bitch!" Molly yells before she kills Bellatrix.[1]

"I love that J.K. Rowling had a mother do this, that it was a mother who put a stop to Bellatrix," I tell my friend.

"I'd like to think I could do that too." my friend says.

"We could," I say, and we watch our girls.

"Bellatrix broke Hadley's heart," I tell her. "She was Hadley's favorite."

My friend tells me her daughter was Bellatrix for Halloween.

"So was Hadley," I say.

I see why Hadley loved Bellatrix. She was fierce. She was strong. She was 100 percent confident in herself. I don't want Hadley to be evil, but I know she admires these traits, and I also don't always know how to show her a fierce, strong, confident woman. I think she sees me more as Mrs. Weasley—a worrier, perhaps a meddler. A gal who asks her if she's aware of how long she's been on her phone and did she eat all of her vegetables.

1. Rowling, *Harry Potter and the Deathly Hallows*, 736.

I watch Harper dribble the ball close to the goal, and I hope that sometimes I can be the good parts of Bellatrix for Hadley, but I also hope Hadley sees that fierceness, strength, and confidence come in many different forms.

Harper scores her first goal.

"I KNEW it, Harper!" one of her teammates yells, and I want to cry seeing the look on this girl's face. She seems as proud of Harper as I am.

Five minutes later Harper scores again. This time it's a stronger, more assured kick.

"She's had a taste," my friend tells me, and we laugh out loud together.

The game ends, and we make our way to our cars, discussing the best routes to take since the other game—the one at the University of Michigan's Big House—is in play. We're not in a hurry today, and I want Harper to tell me all about how it felt to score her first two goals, so I say to Jesse, "Let's see how close to the game we can get." He obliges, and the closer we come to the Big M, the slower the traffic, the louder the roar of the crowd, and the deeper the sea of maize and blue. We roll down windows to hear what's going on, and I stick a hand out of my window to enjoy the fall wind. I can't think of a better place to be in the fall than in a college town. On our way home.

18

The Thunk of Soccer Balls, the Ring of Church Bells

I WAS IN HIGH school, sitting in my youth group pastor's living room with a bunch of other high school kids, and I can't say for sure who was there, but I could make a few guesses. Most of us were girls—kids I'd known since I was six. Boys were active in the youth group too, but this was a Bible study. Something that happened before the pizza and the air hockey, the jokes and the Nightcrossing (the greatest, most wild, most terrifying game you could play in an old Presbyterian church with all the lights off). Boys showed up for that, which was fine with me. I liked the intimacy of this smaller group. I liked that the youth pastor's wife joined us, telling us stories of what it was like being a teenage girl. I liked that we could talk about Psalm 23 and admit how terrifying it was and in the same breath ask for prayers that we'll find a date to Prom.

It was spring, and I can't remember how it came up, but my youth group pastor shared that his daughter, a girl just barely in first grade at the time, had not been invited to a birthday party. He said he wished he could just jump into her skin and feel all her sadness, so that she wouldn't have to.

I bent my legs so I could rest my chin on my knees and looked at my shoes. "That is so dumb," I thought.

Hadley's soccer season has started. On the weekends we un-fold lawn chairs, sit on the sidelines, and watch. Maybe I've seen four games so far, I can't remember, but watching her, I remember with a twinge what my youth group pastor said about his daughter and what I thought in response. While she goes after the ball, I go over the memory in my head, hoping to discover something better than my brutal reaction to a father wanting to hold sadness for his daughter. The best I can come up with is, "Well, Callie, at least you didn't say that out loud."

I understand him now, wanting to take on sadness and frus-tration or whatever hefty thing it is so my kids don't have to.

But I'm also glad I remembered my reaction, albeit disre-spectful, as well, because of its honesty. I worry all the time about my girls being sad, and what it is I ought to do about it. But maybe I should think about how teenage Callie thought about it, and maybe, thirty years later, I can say this: it's not our job to take these things from our daughters.

You know what my youth group pastor was really great at? End-of-the-year slide shows. He'd put together the pictures he'd taken of us all year and set the whole thing to music. Here we are working in Tijuana or New York, pounding nails into walls to build homes for people to live in. Here we are in the youth group room, playing air hockey, a slice of Domino's pizza in one hand and reaching for the puck with the other. He captured memories for us. Here's you in your yellow overalls and your hair with sprayed-to-the-death bangs. Look at you having fun.

He didn't know how hard I was working at fitting in, or the worries I had over homework I didn't understand, or the friends I was trying to make, or the boys I was trying to get over. He didn't need to stand where I was because his clicking the button on a camera and sharing it showed me something else about myself: you are sad, but you are strong. You are confused, but you show up. You are lost, and you are found. All the time you are all these things.

The girls play soccer while church bells ring on Concordia University's campus. The thunk of soccer balls mixes with the hymn's melody.

"Don't watch, girls. Play!" a father yells. That's our job, to watch. You're in the game, ladies. You have to play. We can't do it for you.

So I watch, and I take pictures, and I think about birthday parties and making friends, and trying to get at and then control a ball that is equally fun and frustrating. And I think of Mary, who also couldn't take on all her child took on, but who kept "all these things in her heart." Who kept watching.

19

Safely Graze

AT THE GROCERY STORE Harper and I are standing in line at the self-checkout lane, behind a woman buying 25 loaves of Sara Lee whole wheat bread.

"Jesus Christ," the woman buying the loaves of bread says. She's a small woman, with short white hair, and she's wearing those black good-for-your-feet shoes. I remember my mom got a pair of those shoes and a house dress from her friends on her fortieth birthday. She put them on, and my dad took a picture of her standing on our front lawn in front of a computer printout (probably from a Commodore 64 computer) saying, "Lordie, Lordie, Grace is Forty." I remember standing next to my dad while he took the picture and thinking, "That's funny. My parents' friends are funny."

The woman buying all the bread is angry. Something's wrong with the conveyor belt, or maybe it's the touchscreen. Maybe the grocery store thinks she's buying too many loaves of Sara Lee whole wheat bread and is cutting her off because there won't be enough for everyone else.

"What's she going to do with all that bread?" Harper whispers. "What's she going to make?" Harper says it like it's Christmas morning, and she's just about to open presents. She's proud of this woman, excited at the prospect of what she will do with all these whole wheat loaves of bread.

"I'm not sure," I whisper back, watching the woman figure out her problem. I always have to call for help when I'm having issues with the self-checkout.

I don't want the woman to think I'm annoyed or impatient or some other nasty thing so I look at the magazine covers in the other direction so the woman can be assured I am in no hurry.

On one cover a woman lost all her baby weight in something like seventy-two hours. Her hair is thicker and she finally has everything she's ever wanted. Faith! Fitness! Family! Another woman has figured out how to lose all the menopause weight and also stop the hot flashes and brain fog and moodiness. Her hair is also thicker and she too, has everything she's ever wanted. Happiness! Health! Hope!

"Jesus Christ," I want to say. Instead, I grab a pack of peanut M&Ms and a tube of Maybelline Great Lash Mascara from the shelf and throw them on the conveyer belt. The lady turns at their thud.

"Sorry," I say, palms in the air. I don't understand what I'm apologizing for.

The woman goes back to her bread and I look at my shoes and begin to hum Bach's "Sheep May Safely Graze," based on Psalm 23. It's my default song for when I'm anxious or uncomfortable or scared or annoyed or impatient or ashamed or any nasty thing I don't want to be.

I learned the song around fifth grade when I was in a choir called, "All God's Children." We sang this song in Orchestra Hall on Michigan Avenue in Chicago. We held candles as we sang, and I worried about the flame getting too close to my clothes or the wax dripping onto my fingers. We had to stay very still as we sang, breathing deeply so our voices were heard and also being careful not to get burned. It was a lot to balance—the desire for expression and the fear of pain. When the concert ended, I had a pain in my chest that wouldn't go away. "Something is wrong with my heart," I kept telling my mom.

The lady collects her bread. She's closed a little door on the conveyor belt so that I can run my stuff through while she bags her loaves. I didn't know about that door. I always frantically bag my groceries so the next person doesn't have to wait for me. I hate being a bother, making other people wait for me while I figure something out.

The lady snaps the door shut, looks at me, and nods—my cue to get started.

"Thank you," I tell her, and I know I sound ridiculous, but I tell her I had no clue about this door.

She looks at me and laughs. "You're welcome," she says, and laughs again. She shoves her loaves into bags and then tosses them into her cart while Harper and I scan our groceries: eggs, milk, some clementines, a bag of potato chips, the M&Ms, and a tube of mascara that promises me scandalous lash length.

Harper skips to the end of the conveyor belt, rips a couple of bags off the handles, and begins to put the food and my mascara in them.

"You need a bag for the milk?" she asks.

"Nah," I say, pushing "credit" on the screen.

The woman is still bagging her bread when I join Harper, shoving the receipt in my pocket. I look at the sign above where I scanned my groceries. Usually, these self-checkouts have a limit, twelve items or less. Something like that. Not this one. You can scan all your groceries here. Claim all the loaves of bread you want.

"You need any help?" I ask the lady. She looks at me like I'm nuts.

"It's bread," she says. "No, thanks," she adds and smiles. She has a nice smile.

"Have a good night," I say and take Harper's hand.

Harper's skipping and swinging my arm, so it's tricky to keep balance with the groceries I'm carrying. I think about letting go of her hand but I don't. Instead, I walk with the grace of an ogre who's been at sea for forty days.

This is how we leave the store, me and Harper, while the lady with all the bread brushes past us, having no trouble at all with all she's carrying.

20

Advent in a Church Bathroom

IN THE WOMEN'S BATHROOM at church, there is a border of wallpaper running just below the ceiling with these words: *serenity, home, creativity, simplicity,* and *beauty.* The words are printed in what looks like a medieval font, so there's a seriousness to them, a sacredness. I read them while I'm waiting for a stall, and I wonder if these are words a woman ought to strive for in her pursuit of the life of a Proverbs 31 woman.

Lately I've been writing under a thick blanket of doubt—my yarn weak and ripping, and I don't know if it can be mended together, no matter how much I love it, no matter how much I want to hang on to it. It seems to be disintegrating. Standing here in this church bathroom I'm wondering what *serenity* and *creativity* have to do with each other. I wonder if I will ever obtain *simplicity* in my lifetime. I think I won't if I keep writing.

One woman walks into the bathroom with a cane. "Hello," she says to me, and her smile is so sweet that I want her to tell me everything she knows about *beauty* and *simplicity* and *serenity* and *home.* Tell me everything you know in this small bathroom with the clanging radiator and the frosted windows.

She lifts her cane onto a shelf and says, "Oh, my! These are real!" She turns to me, totally delighted that a handful of sprigs with red berries on them are real. Like, what better thing could there be to know then something is alive? "They're standing in water!" she exclaims.

"They're beautiful," I say, because they are, but I also don't know what else to say. I hadn't noticed the berries. I was ruminating over my lack of *simplicity*.

Another woman walks in, and she goes right to the vase with the berries. "Those are real!" she says, equally pleased, and the two hover over them, not touching the berries, but their hands form a cup shape, as though they are getting ready to hold an infant's head. "What kind of berries are they? Are they holly? No, they can't be holly."

I leave the two of them discussing the red pop of the berries, their voices like young girls at a birthday party who scored the slices of the cake with the frosting flowers, and walk upstairs to where my girls are singing "Light Dawns on a Weary World."

"We shall go out with joy, And be led forth in peace, As all the world in wonder echoes *shalom*." I can hear the music from down the hallway, young voices singing about the arrival of someone notable, someone come to bring us joy and peace and wonder.

Maybe I'm not supposed to figure out what each word has to do with the other. Maybe what it is they have in common is that they point to something alive, and understanding that, I am to say, "This is real!" Delighted and mystified, and echoing the life I see but do not always understand, and nothing more.

21

Filled with Fragrance

I AM IN A Starbucks on Main and Liberty, trying to read and then eventually write about L. M. Montgomery's *Emily Climbs*. Emily, the main character, has just left home for what sounds like a kind of boarding school, one she wants to attend with the same kind of whimsical passion Anne of Green Gables wants a kindred spirit. Emily's Aunt Elizabeth says she'll pay for her schooling, but Emily must give up writing. Emily says absolutely not. Elizabeth says fine, then you must only write what is true—for the rest of her life she must only write what is true. Do this, and she may get an education.

Emily agrees, and she is now in the place she's dreamt of going, but she hates it. It's a dark and scary place with new rules. She wants to go home.

This Starbucks is not the place I want to be either. My first choice was Comet Coffee, but it was packed. Lab, around the corner, was packed too. Further down Liberty, Roos Roast is closed. Bakehouse 46 was busy. I don't like the coffee at Avalon, and while Shinola has the hippest, most glorious coffee shop in its basement, I feel stupid walking inside because I'm not there to buy a very expensive watch—just a very expensive coffee.

So Starbucks it is, and I am more than annoyed. I cannot afford time looking for a place to sit in a coffee shop. I have ninety minutes to write today, and ten of them have been spent searching

64

for a place to sit, which means that another ten will be spent walking back, which leaves me with seventy minutes. Most likely forty of those minutes will be spent staring out the window. Finding the time and space to write is quite literally the story of my life, and the plot is exhausting and relentless.

Two guys walk inside the shop. They're talking about roses. They want to buy them cheap so they can sell them for a profit. "I'm ready to make some cheese," one of them says, and the other one says roses are the way to do this. Roses are how they'll make the cheese.

A third man walks in. He's selling *Groundcover* newspapers. He pulls them out from under his arm and tosses them on the bar table where I'm trying to write. I flinch. The three men laugh. I'm relieved that they're laughing because I know now they won't ask me for money, and if they do, I will feel justified in telling them no because they laughed at me, laughed at my fear. If they ask, I'll just say no. I won't even say sorry.

They don't ask. They get their own coffee, stand behind me, and talk. I read about Emily and her first night at this school that she wanted to go to so much that she promised to only write what was true for the rest of her life, and now she wants to go home. "Father told me once that one could find something beautiful to love everywhere," Emily remembers on this first dark night.

A fourth guy, a boy who looks like he's Hadley's age, sits outside of the Starbucks. He sits at my feet—the only thing separating us is the shop's window. He pulls out a cigarette, lights it, then holds up a piece of cardboard and smoke from his exhale sails up, around and underneath what he's holding.

The newspaper man collects his papers and walks outside, and the rose-men watch him. "He sells papers," one of them says. After a few minutes they leave too.

They don't go anywhere though. The three men surround the smoking boy. One of the rose guys looks at him and smiles. He says something to him and reaches out his hand. They shake.

I watch the newspaper man hand the boy a paper. Under his thumb, atop the news, is a five dollar bill. The boy sees the money and smiles the smile of a child—all wonder and surprise and joy. He stands up, and the newspaper man cups his hand to the boy's face and brings the boy closer to him. He begins to speak to the boy, and the boy nods, then hugs the newspaper man. The rest of us—the rose-guys and me—we watch. We are on all sides of this scene, standing still, watching.

It has begun to rain. The boy sits back down. The men walk away. I pack up my things and throw my coffee cup away.

Outside the world smells of nicotine and rain, of wet cement and gasoline and of a spring that's fighting its way here, like it must every year, and I am afraid to breathe it all in as I make my way back to where I came from.

22

Planting Invisible Faith

1. CLEAR THE GROUND

Oak Park, Illinois. Saturday morning, April 9, 1994.

I HAVE LEFT MY house after screaming at my parents that I'm not going to college. I am 18 and sitting on a bench facing Rehm Park, the playground of my childhood, watching kids dig in the sand, watching them pretend the ground is lava, watching them perform the mighty feat of going up the twirl slide until someone's parent tells them to cut it out.

Last night the world learned Kurt Cobain was dead. I found out at a party where Milwaukee's Best ("the BEEEEAAAAST!") and a goblet of Peppermint Schnapps was being served, and Cypress Hill's "Insane in the Brain" thumped loudly and not in the background. The lyrics pulsed through our lungs, our bloodstream, our souls.

"A bullet to the head! He put a bullet to his head!" one girl wailed.

Kurt Cobain was dead, and my ex-boyfriend walked in with his new girlfriend, the one he dated before me, and I knew exactly which I was more upset about.

"I hated his music anyway," I said, cracking open a beer and, deciding it tasted like pee, reaching for the goblet of Schnapps. "He was always screaming." Really what I mean is I didn't understand his music. Really what I mean is I had a feeling I was the one he was singing about.

Later that night, I took everything my ex-boyfriend ever gave me and set it in his front yard: dried flowers, his letterman's jacket, a giant stuffed bunny rabbit he'd won at a carnival like in some kind of Hallmark movie.

I'm too old to play at this park, but I'm too young to sit on this bench like an old lady waiting for the bus or for pigeons to hop over so she can give them some of her old-ass oyster crackers she keeps in her purse from when she was having soup and pie at Baker's Square. Something needs to happen in this space between childhood and old ladyhood, but I don't know what. Really what I mean is I don't want to find out. Really what I mean is I am afraid.

CONSIDER WHAT TO PLANT

Grand Rapids, Michigan. Calvin College. Winter 1997.

Jesse, my boyfriend, who I know will soon be my fiancé, is in my dorm room during one of three of Calvin's allotted "open house" hours, when girls can go into boys' rooms and vice versa. We must keep our doors open, and there's a "two feet on the floor" rule that is probably some Christian Reformed myth, but the point is at Calvin, we give our hearts to the Lord promptly and sincerely, and we always leave room for the Holy Spirit.

I am reading Mary Shelley's *Frankenstein*, a story I need to read with CliffsNotes, index cards, highlighters and various pens, and a large bag of gummy worms I buy at Meijer from the candy bins (the worms no longer exist, nor do the bins—a heartbreaking shame), and a "Poor Man's Mocha"—coffee and hot chocolate mixed together for fifty cents at "Johnny's," Calvin's snack shop. (Yes, it is named after John Calvin.)

This is how reading is for me. This is how reading always will be. I am slow to understand and quick to be affected by stories. Reading is jumping into Lake Michigan on a June day when the waves have realized they are no longer frozen, and they move with a ferocity from being held still and they rush to shore, knowing part will seep into the sand and part will tug itself into deeper water, eternally changed and changing. I will take an abundant amount of personality and learning tests because as much as I seep myself into the stories I read, as much as I plunge into the depths of them, when I leave the water and I'm asked what it is that happened, I can't answer, thus resulting in a solid C-/D+ assessment of what I know (and let's face it, who people think I am).

"Some people are just not cut out for academics," I am told by people equivalent to Professor Dolores Umbridge.

"And some people are not meant to wear bathing suits, but they do anyway," is what I wished I'd said instead of, "Thank you. Thank you so much for your time." I've learned by now that the world is set up for the Straight A, for the Rule Follower, for the Straight and the Narrow. I'll explore the rest of it. I'll carve out my own damn path.

This is who Jesse will marry, though I don't think he knows it yet. I'm not sure I do either.

Tonight it is the story behind the story that I'm most interested in. Legend has it that Mary and her boys (Lord Bryon, Percy Shelley, etc.) were gathered 'round the fire one dark and stormy night, and they decided to have a ghost story contest. Whoever writes the scariest story wins.

"Mary totally won," I tell Jesse, who is deciding where to pursue his Ph.D. in civil engineering. He's narrowed it down to two schools—both have offered him a full ride and a stipend—University of Notre Dame and the University of Michigan.

He talks to me about the campuses and the neighborhoods. Ann Arbor, he tells me, is a storybook town. He knows I'll love it there. South Bend, on the other hand, is a tad more gritty. He uses the word "industrial."

(Years later my brother will go through a breakup that will leave him confused and sad, and Jesse, in true engineering fashion, will ask him what it is he liked about this girl that left him broken-hearted. "Well," Geoff will say, "we had a lot of fun together."

"Of course you had fun," Jesse will reply. "You're in Chicago! You wanna see if a relationship works, move to South Bend!")

There is a professor at Notre Dame that Jesse wants to work with. He specializes in hydrodynamics—specifically hurricane storm surge—which is what Jesse's interested in. I wouldn't call Jesse a nice guy, but he is a caring one. The way he acts out his concerns is by learning and mastering concepts that will be a part of a solution. I will begin to understand this tonight as he analyzes which school he'll say yes to. I try to listen, but I am thinking about Mary Shelley.

I'm wondering whether she was working out something within herself as the creature Frankenstein made and abandoned lurked outside his house, sobbing for the love he'd never have. Or was she just trying to beat the boys, those poets who think they knew everything? Or was it a bit of both?

I keep reading while Jesse picks up the phone to call Notre Dame and accept their offer.

PREPARE YOUR PLANTING BEDS

South Bend, Indiana. 1999–2004.

We live in an apartment in a building called The Pointe, named after a triangle patch of land bordered by the St. Joseph River and the East Race, a man-made kayaking route. On Saturdays, we walk along the river to the farmers market. We bring home vegetables and sunflowers, and I tell Jesse about the sunflower I planted in my backyard that grew so tall my dad put me on a ladder so he could take a picture of me next to its brown face and yellow pedals.

On Saturdays we also go to the football games, but other times we sit on our balcony and listen to the crowd and guess whether Notre Dame is winning or not.

Tuesday nights we walk to Corby's, the corner bar down the street from us, for $2 pitchers of Leinenkugel that a bartender fills while the music of Maroon Five plays. "This love has taken a hold of me," I sing, while I follow Jesse outside to the picnic tables on nights when it's warm. We talk about what's next—where we'll live, when we'll have kids, how many kids we'll have, careers, houses. We want a boat, too. It's all thrilling. It's all an adventure. It's all doable.

Jesse spends his days (and some nights) at a lab on Notre Dame's campus. He has a giant map of the Gulf of Mexico and part of the Atlantic Ocean that covers his wall and sits above his many computers. He is tracking hurricanes.

Every few months he travels to New Orleans because he is developing a storm surge model for Louisiana to evaluate the levee protection system. Simply put, New Orleans cannot handle a hurricane storm surge of certain proportions, and Jesse and his cohort are attempting to determine this through science and research.

I spend my days (and more nights than I care to admit) at Covenant Christian School, where I teach a split fifth-and-sixth-grade class of twelve. The curriculum is designed around units, and we integrate all the core subjects into those topics. It is an amazing amount of work, teaching this way, but I love looking for and sharing connections and intersections so that my students can see that it all matters, it's all tied together.

One afternoon I come down with a fever that turns into the flu. I am miserable by the end of the school day, but that night, the school is putting on a big Christmas show. My students and I are doing a lip sync and dance routine to Harry Connick Jr's "I Pray On Christmas." (Yes, I choreographed it. Yes, I am dancing with them. Yes, this is 100 percent my idea.)

At home I sip orange juice and swallow ibuprofen while Jesse heats up chicken soup. He knows not to tell me to stay at home. He knows not to say this isn't a big deal. He ladles soup into bowls and hands one to me.

On our drive home from the show, I tell him I feel like a dragon on fire, but I had so much fun.

"When you teach," Jesse says while we drive past campus, toward the river, toward home, "it is like a light switch has been turned on."

I will be at that school for two years before I burn out and go to another one where I'll stay for another two years. This is how it will go for the duration of my teaching career. I cannot stay in any school for more than two years.

I do not know if teaching is a dementor or a patronus.

TEST AND IMPROVE YOUR SOIL

Washington, DC. August 2004.

I have never felt humidity until this night. Humidity does not exist north of the Mason/Dixon line. She is alive and well here, and she feeds on the yankees—those of us who've traveled to our nation's capital, thinking we are going to do so much good. She likes them best, and she's lucky because they're everywhere. In Washington, DC, everyone is here for a specific reason, and that reason is a passion. So she waits on the Metro for one of them to tug at their red tie. She stands outside of Congress, breathing wet and hot air on the sensible yet fashion-forward skirts and white Oxfords, hoping someone will slip and fall while texting on her Blackberry just one more mandate that will set the world right.

She is on the prowl for the Type A, but deep in her uncomfortable soul she knows she'll never devour them. She'll never stop the law-makers, the liberals or the conservatives, anyone who knows precisely what it is they're doing with their lives, and so she comes for the tourists. She glides slowly and stealthily between the monuments, leaving her wet mark on the statues of our forefathers, like the white handprint Saruman the White used to mark the Uruk Hai. She hovers above the Potomac River, steam rising from the water, lurking and teasing those fools thinking, "it's so hot, I'll just have a lemonade by the water." Here is where she'll wrap her victims up in silk and smother them. Humidity is a spider, and Washington, DC is her web.

I am not a tourist, but neither am I a Type-A person. I'm more type D+, but she's coming to devour me too. This is what happens on our first night here, while I try to get two bedrooms, two bathrooms, and one laundry room's worth of stuff into a one bedroom, one bathroom, no laundry room, and a kitchen so small I can't open the oven without hitting the opposite wall apartment. Nothing fits where it is supposed to. There is no room for anything.

I am panicked and raging and wanting Jesse to fix this problem, except he doesn't see a problem. This is where we are now. This is what we chose. This is what Jesse tells me while he sets his computer in our dining/living room/kitchen. He doesn't have time for this, he says. He's working on his dissertation, and he starts a new job in two days.

He starts click-clacking away, and I open my mouth to keep fighting when I realize the click-clacking isn't coming from Jesse. It is coming from a cockroach making its way up our only window.

"I wanna go home!" I yell.

"We are home!" Jesse yells back.

I storm out of the house and into humidity's waiting and hungry arms. She tries, but she does not chew me up and spit me out.

The Beltway, sometime in 2015

I have dropped Hadley and Harper off at school, and I'm driving to meet my friend, Cara, for breakfast before I teach in the afternoon. Once a month we meet to discuss and review our writing. We've been doing this for over five years. We know when to challenge, when to encourage, we've seen each other at our worst, and we've pushed each other to be our best. Cara is the perfect mixture of colleague and friend.

The Beltway reminds me of an eternal assembly line. Around and around we go, circling Washington, DC until we drop ourselves off at an exit. I like that part. You have to know we're you're going, otherwise you just drive around in circles, always on the outside trying to figure out where and how to get in. Not me. Not today. A decade of living here, and I know how to navigate this place. I know where I'm going.

This is when Jesse calls, and when I answer, he sounds cautious, maybe nervous, maybe excited—like a kid who just found five dollars on the sidewalk and isn't sure what to do about it, or if he should do anything at all.

"There's a job," he begins.

Jesse has worked at the National Oceanic and Atmospheric Administration for ten years. It's why we moved here. He is an expert in hurricane storm surge. He is respected, admired, and heartily relied upon.

Here is where we became parents. It's where we've made great friends, where our kids found friends. I became a writer here. I found a job that I love and am good at here.

He tells me the details of this other position. Something about science. Something about water. Ships. Fish.

"It's in Ann Arbor," he says.

"Take it," I say back.

CONSIDER THE PLANT

Oak Park, Illinois. April 9, 1994.

That Saturday when I yelled at my mom and dad and declared "I would not be attending college," I took Betty Smith's *Joy in the Morning* with me. By no means was I a reader by then, but I wanted to stay out of the house for a while. I had no money. I didn't feel like driving anywhere, and in those days cell phones were called car phones and were used for emergencies only. (For example, "Dad? Hi. I'm home, and it's really dark. Can you please, like, come outside and stand here in case there's like a murderer in the garage? Kthx.")

Joy in the Morning is a story about a newly married couple who live in Ann Arbor. It would keep me out of the house and settle me down enough to consider that there is life beyond the Chicago skyline.

I was enamored with Annie McGairy, a girl who didn't think much of herself intellectually, but who loved writing and stories, who stood outside of classrooms at the University of Michigan so she could listen in on the lectures, who didn't fully understand a word until she felt it.

I didn't want to be Annie, but Annie showed me a bit of who I was, and who I might become. When Jesse said, "Ann Arbor," I remembered that eighteen-year-old me who—so scared, so beat down, so sad—found some strength in a story, stood up, and walked toward an adventure.

PICK THE BEST GARDEN SPOT

Ann Arbor, Michigan. 2016 to present.

Three days short of twenty-five years of marriage, Jesse and I wake up to a power outage. A snowstorm the night before took away our heat, our electricity, and left a wind that could slice your throat if you inhaled.

"Coffee. How?" I grumble to Jesse from underneath a thousand blankets.

He reaches for his phone to see the scope of the power outage. "Not York. Not Zingerman's. Not Drip House. Not Roos Roast," he reads me a list of all the coffee places that are *not* open, and it's as long as those parts in the Old Testament where a billion people are begetting each other, and their names are impossible to pronounce so it takes extra long to read and none of it moves the story forward or, in this case, brings me coffee. "Not Starbucks. Not Whole Foods," he keeps going.

I'm going to beat him with a pillow.

The four of us eventually find a place that's open, and set up at a table near a heater. Harper has an algebra final later this week and has brought along some study materials. Hadley is reading a David Sedaris book, something I picked for her for Christmas after she'd come home from school raving about an essay of his. ("How is he so haunting and hilarious?" she asked me. "I have no idea," I said.) Jesse is reading *Braiding Sweetgrass*, also a Christmas present from me.

"This is my favorite chapter," he tells me, pointing to "Burning Cascade Head," and tells me what it's about—water and salmon, science and community. Renewal.

"I hoped you'd like this book," I say.

Harper starts to get frustrated with her work, and Hadley flips over her book and leans towards her. "Harper," she says, "I think I can help." I try not to make it obvious that I'm watching them, leaning against each other, both tapping out equations on paper.

A barista comes over with a tray of pastries fresh from the oven. "On the house," he says, and puts the tray on our table.

With fanfare, gratitude, and delight, as if we are at a wedding, we all take and eat.

This essay first appeared on Coffee+Crumbs,
February 2, 2024

23

For I Know [My] Plans

MORE THAN NEW YEAR'S, it is the anticipation of September that has me inhaling the sweet smell of a freshly sharpened number two pencil and considering all the plans I have for my one wild and precious life.

I will learn to dance on pointe, never mind that I've taken a whopping six weeks of beginning ballet and do not know the difference between a jeté and a dégagé. I will win a Newbery, never mind that I write creative nonfiction, and the book I was supposed to have written years ago is in triage with a pulse so still it might be time to pull the plug.

Nevertheless, September is on its way, and these days I live a twisted version of Jeremiah 29:11: For *I* know the plans I have *for myself.*

Remind us to remember the asymmetry of trees—that it is in growing off balance and uneven that makes them strong.

Remind us of the gruesome work caterpillars must go through when they transform, having no idea what they will become, that they'll emerge with the ability to fly.

Remind us of the cicada, who molts, leaving its paper-like skin on the fence, on our front doors, on our windshields, holding perfectly the shape of what was while the body has flown somewhere else.

Remind us that it was the raven—the scavenger—that went before the dove, searching for peace.

Make us scavengers for peace when the waters are too dangerous and too deep for us. Keep us willing to fly. Make us believe you are with us in our transformation, no matter how gruesome it may be. Let us cling to the belief that we are wonderfully and fearfully made. That no matter how far away we go, the shape of who we are is held safely in Your hands.

24

Some Thoughts on Mystery

I'M NOT A SEEKER of answers. The same is true for definitions and facts. When something has been tangibly and palpably proven, I tend to shrug my shoulders and ask, "What else?"

I prefer to experience the mystery of things. My daughter, Harper, dancing in church on the evening of Ash Wednesday with women she'd called her "new friends," who gently mentored her through not only the steps to the dance, but also what those steps symbolize. She lifted her arms and twirled to words I'm unsure she would not understand if it weren't for the dance and her friends.

I prefer to return to the story. As a pastor explained to Hadley and Harper one winter morning, moments before they would take Communion for the first time. "Every time you take Communion, a different part of you will be ready for it," she said. "Nobody understands all of it. You're stepping into a mystery, and you're standing there for a while."

I prefer to consider the Good Friday service that fell on the same evening as a Michigan spring formal. By then Hadley and Harper were familiar with our drive to church, but they hadn't seen this place nestled in Greek Row in the evening, with twinkle lights and music, red cups and ping-pong tables, girls in fancy dresses and boys in suits. "Is this college?" Hadley gasped, her head as far out of the window as she could get it.

"This is part of it," Jesse told her.

That evening the sanctuary grew darker as the service progressed. Symbols were taken away, put out of sight—no longer could we rely on the music, the words, the objects to guide us through what we were grasping to understand. Hadley and Harper, startled and wide-eyed, watched as the pastors walked silently out of the sanctuary. We were left in the dark, in the silence, in the emptiness.

It was an evening that should've been rainy and murky and cold, but it was warm and bright and the sanctuary's windows were open, and outside a group of boys sang, "Hail! To the victors valiant! Hail! To the conquering heroes!"

Shouldn't they have known? Shouldn't we have told them about the darkness and the silence? Or did they know and sang anyway? Is this also part of the story?

"Try to curb your violent questions," Jeanne Murray Walker writes in her poem, "The Voice,"[1] based on Psalm 46:10 ("Be still and know that I am God"). "Why not believe the beauty you see?"

The beauty of dancing to make words known, the Communion I'm never sure I'm ready to accept but take anyway, the dark and the silence when the church bells are silent, the spring air that arrives unexpectedly, the voices of those who don't question what they've been given, but instead, relish it.

The part of the story I'm looking for and the part of the story that finds me.

1. Murray Walker, *Pilgrim*, .41

25

Before The Story Ends, Faith

I AM SITTING NEXT to Hadley in a hospital room at the University of Michigan. It is Labor Day weekend. Hadley has been a freshman at Michigan for less than a week. Outside, about a block away, students walk the campus and Greek Row. Music bumps. Red Solo cups are everywhere. It is the Friday before the first home game.

Hadley is fighting a kidney infection. The fighting looks like this: extreme chills, extreme heat, vomiting, and pain. So much pain. When the chills come, the nurses bring heated blankets and drape them over Hadley. I stand over her and rub her arms, back, and legs. It is the only thing that makes the shaking stop.

When she gets hot, I rip the blankets off, tear off her socks, and wind her Rapunzel-like hair into a top knot, some pieces already drenched from the sweat. I hold a cold washcloth to her forehead until I feel my palm radiate with her heat. I quickly flip sides, then run to the sink to start it all again.

When it's over and she's sleeping, I fold the blankets. They are thin and beige and linen-like, and it disturbs me when I think they might be similar to the cloth Jesus was buried in, that Mary Magdalene found when the stone was rolled away.

Tonight Hadley's nurse is named Hope. Hope loves Hadley's nails. "They're fresh!" Hope says as she flushes Hadley's IV. Hope, who can't be more than four years older than Hadley, calls her sweetheart, rubs Hadley's feet, cleans up Hadley's vomit as though there's nothing in the world she'd rather do.

I watch the two of them interact and think in another situation, they'd probably be friends. I'd bet on it. Hadley is the friendliest, most effervescent person I've ever met. To see her sick is terrifying, and while I know this is hard on her, I know what's excruciating is being isolated from all the college activity she could not wait to be a part of. Hadley was ready for college in kindergarten.

This is not how the story is supposed to go.

Hope and Hadley are giggling about something I know nothing about, and I'm grateful for this crumb of interaction Hadley is offered. I can tell Hope is too. This is Hadley's magical power—she makes people believe we're all in this together, and what's more, it's fantastic that we're all here, working it out, together. Hadley's faith in the goodness and greatness of people is astounding.

Hope asks what Hadley is majoring in, what dorm she's in and what she thinks of her classes while she takes Hadley's vitals. Her temperature is 103.

"That's really high," Hope says.

No duh, I want to say.

She leaves and Hadley turns to me, crying.

"I hate this," she says.

"I know," I say back. "I hate this too." And that is the end of the conversation. We both hate this situation. There's nothing more to say. The end.

Hadley doesn't want to watch TV or play cards. She doesn't want to do anything to take her mind off how she feels, so we sit in silence and I am forced into Treasuring and Pondering 101. Mary is my teacher. I hate this class.

Three times we are told Mary treasures and ponders her circumstances as the mother of Jesus. The number gets on my nerves. If it were just the one time, maybe even two times, I'd feel fine rolling my eyes and dismissing the line as precious. But three suggests wholeness. It suggests completeness. It suggests God, Jesus, and the Holy Spirit are here in this room, and I ought to pay careful attention to what Mary is telling me about this part of motherhood—the part when we are vessels for a story that is not our own.

A few years ago I went to a funeral for a friend who'd lost her husband. He died suddenly. My friend, newly widowed, also learned she was pregnant.

"Who's writing this story?" one of my friends asked as we stood outside of the church. "Jesus," he added.

He was not answering his question. This was slang, a taunt— tone I am sure Jesus is used to. Tone I believe Jesus considers a call.

"Indeed, this is the plot, as terrifying and devastating and confusing as it is," I imagine Jesus saying back. "And I'm in the story with you. I'm not leaving you."

But I want this story to be over. I want this story to have never happened. Let's swing to another story, Jesus. Let's find treasure there. Please.

Hadley tosses blankets off of her, and I stand, give one a shake, then begin to fold it. I move on to the next, then another, until I've made a neat stack on the counter next to cups of water and jars of applesauce. I pick up one of the cups and bring it to Hadley. She lifts her head slightly and sips through the straw. I watch her, careful not to move because it shifts the straw, and Hadley can't drink without it.

Yesterday, after one too many misses, Hadley said, "Mom, I'm going to make eye contact with you when I'm done drinking so you'll know when to move."

"Okay," I said and offered her the water.

"Just follow the system," she said and closed her eyes so as to give me as little chance as possible not to get confused, a decision I appreciated because I was trying very hard not to laugh at Hadley's command to "follow the system."

She opened her eyes as wide as they could go—again, so there'd be no confusion—and I lost it.

"I'm sorry," I said, but continued to laugh. "Just follow the system," I teased, and then we were both laughing.

Now Hadley lifts her eyes towards me to let me know she's done. There's a hint of humor in her eyes, and I return the look, having faith that humor will carry a path for hope. I take the cup away.

"How about a story?" I ask Hadley, walking over to my bag and picking up *Life of Pi*.

"Okay," she says.

I scooch my chair as close to her as I can get, not even hiding my enthusiasm that I get to read to her like I used to, and also knowing if Hadley had the energy she'd roll her eyes.

"My suffering left me sad and gloomy," I begin and instantly second-guess my decision to pick this book, but I continue because there's nothing else to do. Because Hadley has agreed to listen. Because I want to read her a story.

I don't know how far we'll get. Hadley might get bored. Or she'll get better and we'll pack up and leave this place. For now I'll sit next to her and read the story for as long as she wants. For now we'll keep carefully a story of suffering that leaves us sad and gloomy but hold on to the belief that there is beauty to be found if we're willing to hunt for it. Not the beauty that promises happy endings, or that everything will be okay. The beauty that promises nothing except that it can imprint itself onto all of us, seep its way into everything we do and say and see. It is beauty that will never leave us.

It is my hope this will happen.

And so, we keep reading.

Bibliography

Murray Walker, Jeanne. *Pilgrim, You Find the Path by Walking*. Brewster, MA: Paraclete, 2019.

O'Connor, Flannery. *Mystery and Manners*, New York: Farrar, Straus & Giroux, 1957.

———. *A Prayer Journal*. New York: Farrar, Straus and Giroux, 2013.

Pratt, Mary F. C. "Not Like a Dove." Originally published in *The Other Side*, Spring 2003. https://gladerrand.wordpress.com.

Rowling, J. K. *Harry Potter and the Deathly Hallows*. New York: Arthur A. Levine, 2007.